The Piccolo Bicycle Book

By Richard Ballantine in Pan
Richard's Bicycle Book

Richard Ballantine

The Piccolo Bicycle Book

Piccolo Pan Books

First published 1977 by Pan Books Ltd
Cavaye Place, London SW10 9PG
Reprinted 1977
© Richard Ballantine 1977
ISBN 0 330 25017 5
Printed in Great Britain by
Cox & Wyman Ltd, London, Reading and Fakenham

Contents

1 The world of bicycles

Why are you interested in bicycles? Probably because they are so much fun. Riding a bicycle just feels good: zipping through the park, wind on your face, wheels spinning, lovely swoop as you bank around a bend, a falling rush as you drop down a dip, faster, faster, then shoot up the rise like a roller coaster, light, breathless at the top . . . you can do stunts, like jumping off bumps, or play tag with friends in the yard, or have a race.

Bicycles are also useful: going to the sweet shop, or to school . . . out to the football game . . . visiting friends . . . running down to the brook for a swim . . . and just messing around, hanging about with friends, wherever they are. Bicycles can be

The Artisan

The Lamplighter

found all over the world, from snowy Alaska to the hot Sahara desert of Africa.

Bicycles are good for carrying things. In the Netherlands, where nearly everyone owns a bicycle, many housewives do their shopping by bicycle. In Africa and Asia, farmers load their bicycles with produce for market. With such heavy loads the bicycle has to be pushed, but after the produce is sold the farmer rides home. In Vietnam, during the last war, the North Vietnamese transported their supplies on thousands and thousands of bicycles. In America, a familiar sight is the newspaper delivery boy or girl.

In Great Britain bicycles are used for all kinds of carrying and delivery work. Letters, packages and telegrams are often delivered by bicycle. So are groceries sometimes. You may

The Postman

The Tradesman

even see an onion-and-garlic man, who sells his wares direct from his bicycle. Window-cleaners often still use bicycles, balancing their ladder on a shoulder as they ride.

And of course, all over the world people use bicycles to ride to work or school.

Sometimes people ride just to see the countryside, and because it feels good. Some tourists go out for an afternoon, others take months to ride thousands and thousands of miles. The 1976 Bicentennial Tour in America, for example, covered over 3700 miles from coast to coast!

Cycle racing is a popular sport. Some races are held out-of-doors, like the famous 2400-mile Tour de France, or the Milk Race in England. Hundreds of riders start out together, and the first over the finish line is the winner. Another outdoor race is cyclo-cross, where riders race on a muddy, rocky course, and sometimes have to wade streams or climb steep banks while carrying their bicycles. Indoor races are held on wooden tracks with sharply banked curves. The bicycles used are very light, with no mudguards, brakes or gears, and the riders go fast – sometimes 40 to 60 miles per hour.

Bicycles are popular at circuses. Clowns ride high unicycles, and daring men and women ride cycles on thin wires high in the air.

Bicycles are really useful. They are perfect for short journeys, can do all sorts of work, are easy to ride and simple to maintain. But mostly, they are fun.

2 Which bicycle for you?

You want a bicycle – but what kind ? There are many to choose from. Determining which is best for you depends on what you want to use the bicycle for, what sort of care you want to give it, and your age, size and riding experience. There are four basic types of bicycle :

1 Scaled down roadster with single- or 3-speed hub gears, equal size wheels from 16in to 24in in diameter, general purpose tyres, flat handlebars, and wide saddle. Easy to ride and maintain, the roadster is generally a good first bicycle. It can stand a lot of rough usage, especially in the cantilever frame design, which has a second top tube for extra strength :

Good braking power. Can be fitted with saddlebags and/or panniers for carrying schoolbooks, sports equipment, or even your dog. Suitable for local use and short tours.

2 Hi-riser. Single- or 3-speed hub, or 5-speed derailleur gears. Rear wheel usually larger than front, 20in rear and 16in front a typical combination. Extra tough, knobby tyres. Very high handlebars. Long 'banana' seat, often with a 'sissy' bar at the back.

The hi-riser (widely known as a Chopper, which is the brand name for the Raleigh Industries hi-riser) is a fun bicycle designed for quick handling and stunts. It is not a good first bicycle. Not only is the handling tricky, but in a fall the high handlebars can catch you in the face, or the gear shift lever may hit you in the crotch.

The small wheels make for a stiff, jolting ride, and reduced braking power, especially in wet conditions. A hi-riser has very limited space for carrying things. It is, in short, a trendy, fashionable bicycle which is not of much practical use.

3 Mini-bicycle. Open frame suitable for boys or girls. Single-or 3-speed hub, or 5-speed derailleur gears. Equal size wheels from 16in to 22in in diameter. General purpose tyres. Conventional flat handlebars and a wide saddle.

Mini-bicycles are zesty and fun to ride. Generally more stable than hi-risers, they still have fairly fast handling. Some models come with a quick-release wire basket on the front, and a quick-release hold-all with carrying strap on the back. These are handy for shopping or carrying books or sports equipment. Most mini-bicycles have quick-adjust seat and handlebar height over a wide size range. This allows the bicycle to 'grow' with the rider, or for its use by other members of the family. Suitable for local use and short tours.

4 Scaled down semi-sports or club racer. Lightweight frame. Three-speed hub, or 5- to 18-speed derailleur gears. Equal size wheels from 20in to 24in in diameter. General purpose or high pressure tyres. Downswept handlebars and narrow saddle.

The club sports is the aristocrat of bicycles. It is light, as little as 20 lbs, or about half the weight of a typical roadster. A wide gear range gives excellent hill climbing ability and speed. The riding position may look strange, but is actually the most

comfortable. Braking power is strong. Fitted with saddlebags and/or panniers, the club sports has ample carrying capacity.

These features make the club sports the best machine for long distance riding and touring, and for racing. It needs more maintenance and takes more skill to ride than other types of bicycle, but is the most exciting and satisfying type to use.

We've covered the different types of bicycle. Now match this information to your own needs. What do you want a bicycle for? If you live in the country and are going to ride a lot in fields and down rough tracks, your best bet is probably a roadster, perhaps with a cantilever frame. Or are you mostly interested in riding in schoolyards and other paved areas, making lots of turns, playing games of tag? A mini-bicycle or hi-riser is best for this, but be aware that you will pay a price; these bicycles are not so good in traffic, or for longer trips. Do you want to look sharp and fashionable? The hi-riser is modelled after a combination of dragster and motorcycle and looks impressive – sitting still. A race with a club sports will leave you eating dust.

Are you interested in longer trips – to and from school, visiting friends, touring at weekends and holidays – possibly even racing? Then a 5- or 10-speed club sports is the machine you need.

How much care and attention do you want to give your bicycle? Does the idea of maintenance bore you? Do you know the difference between a bolt and a screw? Are you going to leave your bicycle out in the rain? Let it fall down on the ground when you are not using it? Be realistic. Lots of people prefer a trouble-free bicycle that can take knocking around. If this is how you feel, get a roadster, mini-bicycle or hi-riser.

Do you like fiddling around with mechanical gadgets? Have you handled tools a little bit? Are you prepared to give your bicycle some care and attention – keep it clean, make occasional adjustments? You'll probably find a club sports the most rewarding.

Before making a final choice, read the chapters in this book on riding and touring for more information on what you can do with different types of bicycles. Try out some bicycles if you can. Friends may give you rides. If you join a cycling club (more on this later) there is almost sure to be someone who will loan you a machine. You can often rent bicycles in towns. If you are dealing with a friendly bicycle shop that knows you are serious about buying a bicycle, they may loan you one for a day or two.

The performance, comfort, and practicality of a bicycle are affected by its parts, such as the gears, brakes, wheels, handlebars and saddle.

Gears

There are three basic types of gears: none, or 1-speed; internal hub gears in 3- to 5-speeds; and derailleur gears in 5- to 18-speeds.

1 Single-speeds are simple and durable. They require no maintenance beyond regular lubrication. They are also hard pedalling going up hills, and offer little speed on the flat. Single-speeds are practical only where the land is flat, such as in the Netherlands.

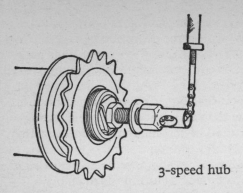

3-speed hub

2 Internal hub gears are extremely reliable. They are well protected against falls and dirt. With regular lubrication and an occasional simple adjustment they will last a lifetime. Changing gear is simple and easy, and can be done at any time. Range is good, with gears for hill climbing, general use and speed.

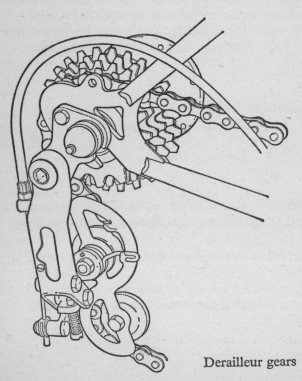

Derailleur gears

3 A derailleur system has the gears, called sprockets or cogs, outside the hub. To change gear, the derailleur moves the chain from one cog to another. This system allows a very wide gear range, with super-low gears for climbing the steepest hills, and high gears for the most speed.

A derailleur system requires regular maintenance, and must be treated with more care than an internal hub gear. Letting the bicycle fall to the ground, or bashing the gear mechanism against rocks or trees, will cause damage.

Derailleur gears are more difficult to operate than hub gears. Changing can be done only whilst pedalling, and usually requires taking your hand off the handlebars.

Summing up

Unless you live in a flatland area, forget about single-speeds. Internal hub gears are reliable, durable and easy to operate, making them a good choice for the beginner rider, for lots of stop-and-go riding or for rough use and casual care. Derailleur gears are the best for long distance travel and touring, or racing. They give maximum performance, but need some care and attention.

Brakes

There are two basic types: the coaster, which is foot-operated, and the calliper, which is hand-operated. Sometimes a bicycle will be equipped with both types.

1 Coaster brakes should be used only by those with too weak a grip to operate calliper brakes. Coaster brakes are given to locking up the rear wheel, causing a skid which not only lengthens the stopping distance, but may cause a fall. To stop, you must first reverse the pedals. This may take too long in an emergency.

On long, downhill rides a coaster brake can burn out. The one advantage of the coaster brake is that it stops well in wet conditions.

2 Calliper brakes come in side- or centre-pull designs.

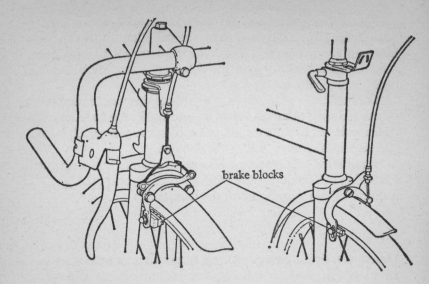

brake blocks

Centre-pull brakes are better than side-pull brakes. They work evenly, and stop quickest.

Calliper brakes do not work well in wet conditions, needing up to five times the distance for a stop in the dry. Some makes are better than others in this respect. Good brands are Campagnolo, Shimano, Mafac, Dia-Comp, Universal and Weinmann.

Saddle and handlebars

Choice of saddle affects
choice of handlebars,
and vice-versa.
There are two types of saddle:

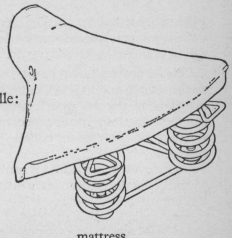

mattress

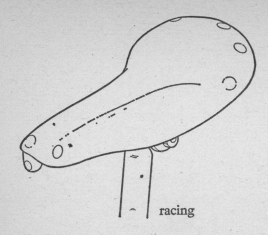

racing

The mattress saddle is made for use with flat handlebars. It has springs because it must support all of the rider's weight. Racing saddles are used with dropped handlebars and are long and narrow to minimize friction between the legs. They do not need springs because the rider's arms help support his weight. The racing saddle used with the dropped handlebar is the most efficient and comfortable. It offers the greatest variety of riding positions, lets you develop the most power, and takes bumps the best. With a mattress saddle you sit straight and each bump rams right up your spine. Your whole upper body is lifted. On a racing saddle you pivot at the hip with each bump. Your spine is not compressed, much less of your body is lifted, and the ride is therefore much more comfortable.

Saddles are made of leather or plastic, or both. Leather saddles need about 500 miles of riding before they are comfortable, but then the fit is perfect. Plastic saddles need no breaking in, but become slippery with your own sweat in warm weather. Plastic saddles are lighter, and are often used in short distance races.

Hi-rise handlebars and banana saddles are worthless. You'll never see them in a race or on a long tour. With hi-rise handlebars your arms cannot support any of your weight. Instead, you have to waste energy holding your arms up! Set at face level, in a fall hi-rise handlebars can catch you in the face. Forget about hi-rise handlebars. They are useless and dangerous.

A very important consideration in choosing a bicycle is your size. A bicycle must fit you, like a pair of shoes. This book has an entire chapter devoted to the subject of fitting. Read it before you choose a bicycle.

Some general advice: get the best bicycle you can afford. Go for quality, not features. It is better to get a quality 5-speed than a cheap 10-speed. Good quality, comfortable saddles and ball-bearing equipped pedals are signs of quality.

In club sports bicycles, the models of the smaller manufacturers, who specialize in this sort of product, are generally of better quality than the products of the larger manufacturers.

Recommended bicycles

I've not given the retail prices of the bicycles listed below because the information would be out of date by the time you read this. Each bicycle listed is a sound machine and good value for the money.

Roadster bicycles

Cantilever frame
Raleigh 'Tempo'. 15-in frame, 20-in wheels. Single speed. Side-pull brakes. Colour: green. Suit inside leg measurement of 23½in to 26½in.

Puch 'Mini-Sprint'. 14½-in frame, 20-in wheels. Single speed. Side-pull brakes. Colour: boys – purple or red; girls – blue or bronze. Suit ages 7 to 10.

Conventional frame
Raleigh 'Chicco'. 14-in frame, 20-in wheels. Single speed. Side-pull brakes. Colour: yellow. Suit inside leg measurement of 20½in to 24in.

Raleigh 'Rodeo'. 16-in frame, 20-in wheels. Single speed. Side-pull brakes. Colour: blue. Suit inside leg measurement of 22½in to 26in.

Raleigh 'Rebel'. 16-in frame, 24-in wheels. Single speed. Side-pull brakes. Colour: tangerine. Suit inside leg measurement of 25in to 28in.

Puch 'Calypso'. 18-in frame, 24-in wheels. Three-speed hub gears. Side-pull brakes. Colour: bronze. Suit inside leg measurement of 27in to 30in.

Raleigh 'Jeep'. 18-in frame, 24-in wheels. Three-speed hub gears, or single-speed. Side-pull brakes. Colour: single-speed – yellow; 3-speed – red. Suit inside leg measurement of 27in to 30in.

Mini-bicycles

Dawes KP18 Junior Kingpin. 14-in frame, 18-in wheels. Single-speed. Side-pull brakes. Colour: red, blue, green, or purple. Suit ages 7 to 11.

Dawes KP500 Kingpin. 17-in frame, 500A wheels. Three-speed hub gears. Side-pull brakes. Colour: blue, purple, brown, or green. Suit ages 11 and up.

Raleigh 'Commando'. 18-in studded tyres. Three-speed hub gears. Side-pull brakes. Colour: black, amber, or pink. Suit ages 7 to 11.

Hi-riser

Raleigh 'Chopper'. 15½-in frame, 16-in front wheel, 20-in rear wheel with studded tyre. Seat shocks. Three-speed hub gears, or 5-speed derailleur gears. Side-pull brakes. Colour: lemon, red, violet, or pink. Suit ages 10 to 15.

Moto-cross

New from Raleigh are the Grifter, Stika and Boxer bicycles. Very robust, and with heavy studded tyres, these are designed for off-road use in woods and fields. This kind of riding can be great fun, but the bikes are very heavy for road use, and the studded tyres skid easily on wet pavement.

Moto-cross bicycles with shock absorbers are not yet easily available in England. Chessington Cycles, Oakcroft Road, Chessington, Surrey KT9 1SA has announced they are importing the Yamaha 'Moto-Bike'. Write to them for particulars. Trusty Manufacturing Co, Cranborne Road, Potters Bar, Hertfordshire EN6 3JS are considering importing the American Matthews moto-cross bicycles. Write and ask for details.

Club sports bicycles

Small
Trusty 'Capri'. 16½-in frame, 20-in wheels. Three-speed hub gears. Side-pull brakes. Colour: red. Suit minimum inside leg measurement of 24in.

Medium
Falcon Model 58 Junior Racer. 18-in frame, 24-in wheels on small flange hubs. Five- or 10-speed derailleur gears. Alloy handlebars, stem, and side-pull brakes. Colour: yellow or red.

Dawes Model 18 Red Feather. 18½-in frame, 24-in wheels on small flange hubs. Five-speed derailleur gears. Alloy handlebars, stem, and side-pull brakes. Colour: gold or red.

Peugeot Junior Sports G45 CME. 18-in frame, 24-in wheels on high flange hubs. Five-speed derailleur gears. Alloy Mafac centre-pull brakes. Colour: violet or orange.

Eddy Merckx Junior Racer Model 112. 18-in frame, 24-in wheels on small flange hubs. Five- or 10-speed derailleur gears. Alloy handlebars, stem, and side-pull brakes. Colour: orange or white.

Large
Falcon Model 70 Black Diamond. 19½-in frame, 26-in wheels on large flange hubs. Alloy handlebars, stem, and centre-pull brakes. Alloy cotterless crankset. Five- or 10-speed derailleur gears. Colour: white, silver, red, or purple.

Falcon Model 64. As model 70 above, but small flange hubs and steel cottered crankset. Colour: yellow or blue.

Dawes Streak Model 22. 19½-in frame, 26-in wheels on small flange hubs. Five-speed derailleur gears. Alloy handlebars, stem, and side-pull brakes. Colour: cerise, geranium, or black.

Dawes Chevron Model 20. As model 22 above, but with five- or 10-speed derailleur gears. Colour: blue, aquamarine, yellow, or silver.

The Bickerton

This is a bicycle newly available, weighing only 18 lb, which can be folded down to the size of a small suitcase in less than 45 seconds. It will fit into the boot of a Mini. The compactness and lightness of the Bickerton make it easy to store in homes with limited space, and to take on holiday. A large canvas carrier bag provides ample space for books and sports equipment, and is also used to carry the bicycle when folded. The bicycle is made of aluminium alloy, so there is no worry about scratched paint or rust. Performance is excellent.

Priced at over £100, the Bickerton seems to be expensive as a child's bicycle. However, between the ages of 9 and 18, a youngster will require three or four different-sized bicycles, each costing £40 or more. The Bickerton adjusts in size to suit from children right up to 6ft 2in adults, and thus in the long run is more economical. Additionally, it can be used by any other members of the family.

The Bickerton is a true lightweight and is not suitable for cross-country bashes or jumping on and off kerbs. It would not be a good choice as a first bicycle. This limitation aside, the unique capabilities of the Bickerton make it worth very careful consideration. For further information, write to

Bickerton Bicycles Ltd
84 Brook Street
London WIY IYG

Cycling Paris.

VIGOR'S
"Our Little Ones."

THE thousands of parents, guardians, and others who have patiently and impatiently waited the coming of Children's Bicycles are this year congratulating themselves that they did wait.

Never in the History of Cycling

have such superb and dainty little machines as

VIGOR'S
"Our Little Ones"

been offered to the Public. These perfectly constructed bicycles are

FIRST CHOICE THE WORLD OVER,

and Children are delighted with them.

Light and Strong.

Cash Price, **£10.**

MADE OF THE FINEST TUBING.

STRONG AS ANY ADULTS' MACHINES.

FITTED WITH ALL LATEST IMPROVEMENTS.

FOR BOYS AND GIRLS.

Order at once, or send for Illustrated Catalogue to

Vigor & Co. 21, Baker St., London.

3 Buying a bicycle

You're buying a bicycle! If you know about bicycles, or have learnt the basic information in this book, you are capable of doing this on your own. But most likely your parents are involved. They should be. First of all, a bicycle is not just a harmless toy. Every year, thousands of children and adults are badly hurt or killed in cycling accidents. Your parents need to know that you are, or can be, a skilled and safe rider.

Secondly, your parents are involved because they are most likely providing the money to buy the bicycle. They will want to make sure that the £20 to £60 spent for a bicycle is wisely invested. Their experience is useful. Still, it is *your* bicycle. You're the one who is going to ride and take care of it, perhaps for many years, so I hope you have a lot to do with buying it.

Often a parent likes to make the gift of a bicycle a surprise. This is very nice, but can result in a bicycle which is not quite right for you. Your bicycle needs to fit you and your needs, like a pair of shoes or pants. This fitting can only be done by your going to the shop. So if the gift must be a surprise, I hope it is in the form of a gift certificate which allows you and your parents to go to the shop and select your bicycle together.

Incidentally, this is a good time to point out that, besides being fun to ride, a bicycle is the cheapest transportation going. It even beats walking! Several hundred or a thousand miles will do for a pair of shoes, but the wear and tear on a bicycle over the same distance is negligible. In fact, a bicycle easily pays for itself. Work out how much you spend each year for trains and buses. The chances are that it comes to no more than the price of a bicycle.

The best place to buy a new bicycle is a bicycle shop. A shop will help select a bicycle suitable for your needs. They will assemble it for you, and while you must check their work, the chances are your new bicycle will work properly. If any problems do arise, the shop is available to fix them right away. Replacement parts are right to hand. You get a guarantee, usually for a year. And you'll find that you want to deal with a bicycle shop anyway, for servicing, parts, accessories, and advice.

Taking delivery

I have purchased many new bicycles, and there was something wrong with nearly every one. A few I rejected outright. So avoid the temptation to pedal merrily away on your new machine. Spend time on a careful inspection. You may save yourself a lot of trouble. Here is the procedure:

◉ Check the frame for straightness. Stand behind or in front of the bicycle and see that the wheels are in line. Next, hold the bicycle by the saddle only and wheel it around the shop. If the frame or forks are bent, it will tend to veer to one side. Finally, if you do a test ride, at some point when you are clear of traffic hold the handlebars as lightly as possible, even riding hands off if you have this skill. The bicycle should go straight, in control, without pulling to one side. Reject any bicycle which fails these tests. A bicycle which will not track accurately is tiring and unsafe to ride.

◉ Check the finish for blemishes, wrinkles or bare spots. Check that welds where tubes are joined are even and complete.

◉ Check that every nut, bolt and screw is tight and secure. After you have ridden 50 miles or so, repeat this operation. New bicycles 'bed down' and must be tightened up – or you will find bits and pieces falling off.

◉ Wheels should spin easily, and be centred in fork arms or chain stays. Check that the rim is true by holding a pencil braced on a brake next to the rim and spinning the wheel. It should not move from side to side more than $\frac{1}{8}$ inch (3 millimetres). Check wheel bearings by holding the bicycle firmly and pushing wheel from side to side. If there is a clicking noise, the bearings are out of adjustment. Pluck the spokes. All should be evenly tight and give the same 'twang'.

◎ Brake blocks should hit rims squarely and not drag when released.

◎ Hold the front brake tight and rock the bicycle forwards and backwards. If there is a clicking sound, the headset may be out of adjustment, or the brake mounted loosely.

◎ Gears should work smoothly and without slipping. Test first with wheels off ground and then on a ride.

◎ Pedals and chainwheel should spin easily, but without side-to-side play.

◎ Finally, ride the bicycle for two or three miles. Make sure everything works, and listen for funny noises.

Secondhand bicycles

Buying a secondhand bicycle is a good way to save money. Use the tests above to check the condition of any machine you consider purchasing. You will not have the protection of a shop guarantee, so inspect it carefully. Before you inspect, read the chapter in this book on maintenance and repair. Often a secondhand bicycle needs some work or new parts. You should know how much it will cost and how difficult it will be.

When you inspect a secondhand bicycle, try to find out how the previous owner treated it. Do you think he or she was interested in their bicycle and took care of it? Pay particular attention to the frame. Look for wrinkled paint on the forks, and where the top and down tubes meet the frame. These can indicate a collision which bent the bicycle. A certain number of nicks and scrapes are inevitable, but there should be no major dents or rust. Be suspicious of new paint.

Incidentally, a secondhand bicycle is often good for learning to ride. You need to be able to touch the ground with both feet whilst sitting on the saddle, and the bicycle may be a little small for you once you have learnt to ride. If you've started on a simple, inexpensive machine, then you can move up to a better bicycle more quickly.

Sources: You may have friends who are ready to sell their bicycles. Some bicycle shops sell secondhand machines. The publications *Exchange & Mart* and *Cycling* carry adverts for secondhand bicycles, and so do local newspapers. Jumble sales, auctions, and street markets are good sources. Newsagents' windows and school notice boards occasionally have adverts, and you can even put up some of your own:

BICYCLE WANTED

3 – SPEED   19" FRAME

GOOD CONDITION

PLEASE RING PETER 170 6918 (AFTER 4 PM)

Building your own

You may have very little money, or want to ride a bicycle you have built yourself; if so, you can assemble your own bicycle – from scrap. I've got a nice little 1952 Triumph that came off a scrap heap. Four pounds fifty pence spent on reconditioning – new chain, cables, tyres, ball bearings and a tin of paint – and it was ready for the road. If you're willing to put in the work, you can do the same. Naturally, the more familiar you are with servicing a bicycle, the easier this job will be. Building from scratch is good for a beginner, because there is no better way to learn exactly how a bicycle works.

Before commencing work, I suggest you read a complete repair manual, such as my *Richard's Bicycle Book* (Pan, £1.25). Then start to scrounge for parts. The more complete a cycle you can find, the better. But most likely you'll have to build up with bits and pieces. Junkyards and rubbish heaps are good places to look. Ask around your neighbourhood. Perhaps someone has an old bicycle mouldering in a shed. Cycle shops often have old wrecks which you can have for very little or nothing. You'll have to make do with what you can find, but get the best frame you can, and make sure it has not been badly bent.

Once you have got all the bits and pieces together, clean them up. Use a wire brush and sandpaper to remove all rust. Undercoat and paint the frame and forks. Then – go to it!

Keeping your bicycle

Once you have got your bicycle, make sure you keep it. Security measures depend on where you live. In many places you can safely leave your bicycle unlocked while you play, go into a newsagent's, or whatever you like. In other areas you cannot: this is for you to judge. Having your bicycle stolen is depressing, upsetting – and expensive. A lock can prevent this.

For ordinary use I find that a light cable combination lock such as those sold in bicycle shops is the most convenient. If you live in a bad neighbourhood or leave your machine unattended for long periods of time, use a length of heavy chain – you can buy this from an ironmonger – and a good quality, case-hardened padlock. A convenient way to carry this is wrapped around the seat post with the padlock shackled to the rear of the saddle. Prevent rattling by encasing the chain in an old tyre tube.

When locking up

⊙ Lock to immovable objects like lamp posts, parking signs, parking meters, heavy fences, etc.

◎ Run the chain or cable through the frame and front or back wheel, both wheels, if you can. Always lock through the frame. Wheels and racks are easily removed.

◎ Try to pick busy places with lots of people and lights. Putting your bicycle 'out of the way' in a dark alley makes a thief's job easier.

◎ If there is somebody around – a newsagent, a flower-seller, a cinema cashier, whoever – ask them to keep an eye on your bicycle.

◎ Keep a written record of your bicycle make, model, size, colour, and serial number – most often stamped on the underside of the bottom bracket, but sometimes found on a stay or tube.

Insurance

A variety of insurance services are available for the cyclist. Membership of the Cyclists' Touring Club (see pp. 59–63 for details) automatically includes third party insurance to the value of £250,000. This means that if you are in an accident and hurt someone, or damage property, the insurance company will pay any claim against you up to £250,000. Also available, for a modest fee, is insurance against theft, or damage to your bicycle.

Cyclist insurance services are available privately from Crusader Insurance Company Ltd, Reigate, Surrey, RH2 8BL, who will send a leaflet on request. Insurance is also available privately through many bicycle shops.

4 Fitting

For you to get the most out of a bicycle, the frame must be the right size, and the saddle, handlebars and controls must be correctly positioned. A bicycle must fit you, like a pair of shoes. Otherwise it will be uncomfortable, and no fun to ride.

Frame

If you are getting a bicycle on which you will learn to ride, you must be able to touch the ground easily with both feet while sitting on the saddle:

If you know how to ride, the top tube of the frame should just come up to your crotch when you straddle the bicycle. This is the simplest way to size a frame. If you are dealing with a bicycle with 26-in or 27-in wheels you can also use these formulae:

1 Your height in inches divided by three. Example: you are 5 feet tall. Five feet equals 60 inches. Divided by 3 equals 20 inches. This is the size of frame you need.

2 Your inside leg measurement taken in stockinged feet from floor to crotch, less 9 inches. Example: your measurement is 28in, less 9in, equals a 19-in frame.

Saddle

The springiness of some saddles can be adjusted by turning nut A:

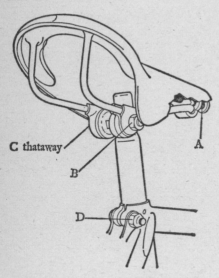

To remove the saddle from the seat post, or to move it forward or backward, or to tilt it, loosen nuts B and C. To raise or lower the saddle, loosen the binder bolt D. Always leave at least 2in of the seat post inside the seat tube.

On hi-risers equipped with banana saddles, an additional adjustment may be necessary to the 'sissy' bar.

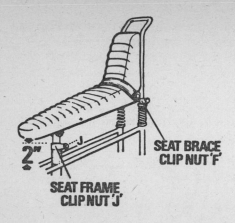

SEAT BRACE CLIP NUT 'F'

SEAT FRAME CLIP NUT 'J'

2"

Most saddles are set too low. A rough rule of thumb is that when you are sitting on the bicycle with your heel at its lowest point, your leg should be straight.

A better way to find the correct saddle height is to measure in inches the inside length of your leg from crotch to floor without shoes. Multiply this figure by 1·09. Example: 32in × 1·09 = 34·88 or 34⅞in. Set the saddle so that distance A from the top of the saddle to centre of pedal in down position is 34⅞in:

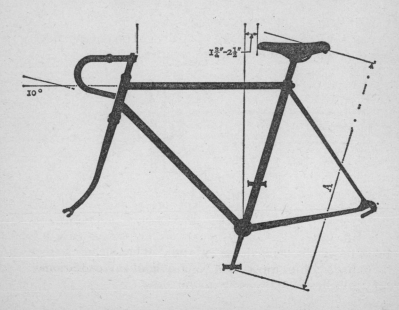

The correct fore to aft position for a saddle is between 1¾in and 2½in behind a vertical line through the bottom bracket (see previous illustration).

Handlebars

Handlebar height is adjusted by moving the stem. Undo the expander bolt E a few turns:

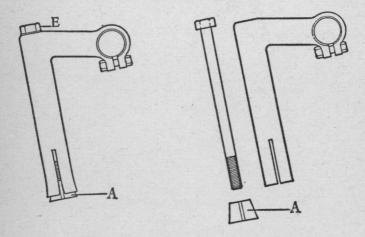

Place a block of wood or piece of cardboard on the expander bolt to protect the finish, and tap it with a hammer:

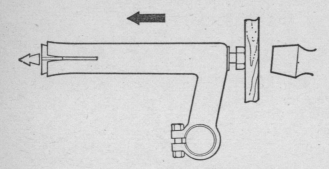

Repeat as necessary to get stem loose. Set handlebars so that they are level with the saddle. Keep at least 2in of the stem inside the head tube.

If you have downswept handlebars, set the ends 10° from the horizontal:

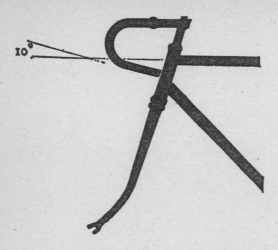

To adjust handlebars, loosen binder bolt A on stem:

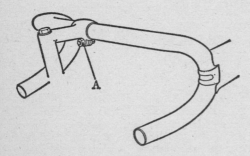

Brakes

To adjust the position of a brake lever on flat handlebars, loosen the bolt or screw B:

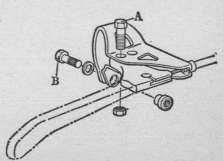

On downswept handlebars, loosen the bolt or screw A:

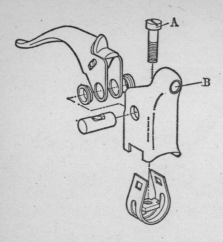

You will have to hold down the brake lever while you do this. Position the brake levers so that you can operate them from above:

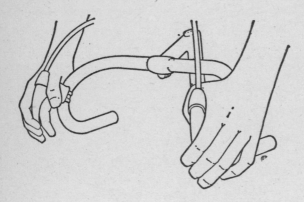

Gearing

This is too difficult to cover here, but if you have a derailleur gear bicycle for general use and touring, make sure it is equipped with wide-ratio gears, and if you are going racing, have close-ratio competition gears.

5 Riding

You can learn how to ride a bicycle by yourself, without any help. Do not use training wheels. You must learn how to balance, and training wheels make this difficult.

Adjust the saddle (see p. 34) of your bicycle so that you can touch the ground comfortably with both feet when mounted:

MOUNTING.

DISMOUNTING.

Find a piece of gently sloping, open ground in a park where
there are no cars, point the bicycle downhill and climb on.
Check the brakes. Now push along with your feet, as if you were
on a scooter. Use your feet to keep your balance. Do not try to
pedal. If you go too fast, apply the brakes gently.

An hour or two of this 'scootering' will teach you how to
balance and turn a bicycle. Now try longer 'scoots', resting your
feet on the pedals. In a short while you will be able to ride down
a hill with your feet on the pedals, turning when and where you
want, and controlling speed with the brakes.

Now place the gears in 1st or L (see *Shifting*, below). Start
by scootering, place feet on pedals, and pedal. It's that easy!

Spend the next few sessions just riding around your practice
area. A bunch of cardboard boxes spaced apart in a line makes a
good course. Practise stopping quickly. Keep the following
basics in mind:

Pedalling

Ride with the ball of your foot on the pedal, not the heel or arch. Try ankling. Start at the top of the stroke with the heel slightly lower than the toes. Push with ball of foot and at the same time pivot at the ankle so that the foot levels out half-way down, and finishes with the toes lower than the heel:

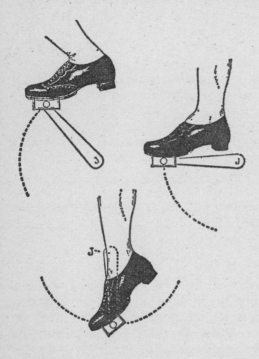

Cadence

This is the speed at which you pedal. Most people pedal too slowly and push too hard. It is much better to pedal rapidly. Use your gears to maintain a fast pedalling rate. Shift just before you come to a hill.

Shifting

Make your first shifts slow and deliberate. Once you have learnt the knack, fast gear changes will be easy.

Hub gears: 1 or L is low gear, for hills, 2 or M is second gear, for general use, and 3 or H is high gear, for speed. To shift gear, ease up on pedals, move the selector to desired gear, resume pedalling. If the bicycle is standing still, back-pedal a little as you move the selector.

Derailleur gears: shift these only while you are pedalling. To see why, hang your bicycle so that the rear wheel is up off the ground, rotate the cranks, and manipulate the gear levers so you can see how the chain moves from cog to cog. Shifting without pedalling can bend or break the chain or gear teeth.

The shift levers do not have stops for the various gears and you have to learn where they are by feel. Get under way, ease pedalling pressure but do not stop pedalling, and gently move the gear lever until you feel the gears shift. Do not let the derailleur cages rub the chain. This is shown by a steady whirring/clicking noise that stops if you stop pedalling. Move the shift lever just a little and the noise will stop.

Do not run the chain from the big front sprocket to the big rear sprocket, or the small front sprocket to the small rear sprocket. It causes the chain to cut across at too severe an angle, greatly increasing wear.

Braking

Try to be sparing in your use of the brakes. This will help you to look ahead and know what problems you may encounter. Be careful of braking too hard and skidding. Use both front and rear brakes together, and apply the front brake gently. On some bicycles the front brake is very strong so that if you put it on hard, you may be pitched head-first over the handlebars. In slippery conditions or when banking over for a corner, use the rear brake. The rear wheel has a slightly greater tendency to skid, but if it goes you may still be able to stay upright, and at worst will land on your hip. A front wheel skid, however, will dash you on your face and injure you seriously.

Practise braking until it is second nature. Know exactly the distance in which you can stop. In an emergency there is no time to make this sort of calculation, or wonder which brake lever does what.

In rain or wet conditions apply the brakes lightly and often. This wipes water off the brake shoes and wheel rims, and greatly increases braking power. For a complete stop, fully wet brakes and rims take four to five times the distance needed for a stop in dry conditions.

When coasting down long hills, avoid overheating the brake shoes by pumping (on-off-on-off-on-off) the brakes. Always be able to stop!

Bumps

When you come to bumps, potholes, rough ground, etc. put most of your weight on the pedals and handlebars, even lifting your behind clear of the saddle. This allows the bicycle to pivot underneath you, reducing shock. Do not ride your bicycle on and off kerbs. It is very hard on the tyres, wheels, and wheel bearings.

Mechanical control of a bicycle is easy to learn. But you must also know how to ride on streets and highways shared with motor vehicles. This takes a lot of knowledge, skill, and attention. Each year many cyclists are killed or maimed in accidents. Knowing how to ride properly reduces your risk of accident enormously, but it takes time to learn – don't rush it.

The most important thing to understand about cycling in traffic is that it requires all your attention. The street or highway is not the place for fun riding – save that for parks, schoolyards, and country fields. In traffic you must be aware of everything that is happening, from the size of the pebbles on the road to the number and type of vehicles before and behind you – absolutely everything. Start playing, drop your attention for a moment or two, and you may die.

I want you to understand clearly the importance of alertness. It is possible that you have done some dangerous things, or been hurt in some sport or accident. Bruises, a twisted ankle, perhaps a broken bone – that sort of thing. In traffic, one wrong move can see you rolled up underneath a car in seconds. I hope you find this frightening. Riding in traffic is dangerous. Really dangerous! Plenty of grown-ups who will drive cars at 70 mph and more will not cycle in traffic. Unless you live in an area which provides cyclepaths, you do not have a choice. It is ride in traffic or not at all.

If you decide to ride in traffic you have good reason to be constantly watchful. However, with some practice, you will still be alert, but relaxed. For example, crossing a street is dangerous, but once you have learnt to do it, you are more relaxed. It is much the same with cycling in traffic.

Your first step is to enrol in the National Cycling Proficiency Scheme, which trains and tests people in cycling and the Highway Code, the book of basic rules for all users of the road. The Scheme is free and takes only a few hours to complete. Inquire at your school or police station for details.

As part of the course you will have to study the Highway Code. It is available from Post Offices and bookshops. Read and study it carefully. It is important that you understand the rules of the road for both yourself and for other road users. In general, the rules for a cyclist are:

◉ that you ride as well to the left as you can;
◉ obey traffic signs, lights, and the directions of traffic wardens;
◉ give way to pedestrians at zebra crossings;
◉ signal turns and stops.

Always stay as far to the left as you can. Do not ride in the centre of the road even if there is no other traffic about. A car can arrive very quickly. Keep to the left, but keep a lookout for debris, stones, water drains, broken glass, and other hazards that may be near the edge of the road. When passing parked cars, leave enough room to allow for a car door opening in your path:

If you need to swing out to clear a parked car, do so well *before* coming to the parked vehicle:

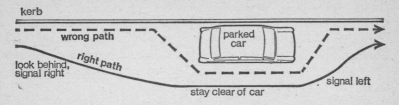

Obey traffic signs. You'll find a complete list of these in the Highway Code. Here are a few:

Turn Left Ahead (Right if Arrow is reversed)

Keep Left (Right if Arrow is reversed)

Route for Cyclists (Compulsory)

Warning Signs mostly Triangular

Steep Hill Downwards

Level Crossing without Gate or Barrier Ahead

Obey traffic lights. Red means stop. Red and amber also mean stop. Flashing amber is proceed if you have a clear way. Green means go. A green arrow means you can go in the direction of the arrow.

Obey police signals. The six basic signals are:

STOP

1 Vehicles approaching from behind

2 Vehicles approaching from front

3 Vehicles approaching from both front and behind

GO

4 Beckoning on a vehicle from front

5 Beckoning on a vehicle from behind

6 Beckoning on a vehicle from the side

Signal all stops, starts, and turns:

Move left

Move right

Slowing down

The proper way to get moving on a bicycle is to start from the left kerb. Bring the off-side pedal around to the 2 o'clock position. Look behind and check traffic. Then pull away.

When making a left turn, check traffic behind, then signal. Do not swerve out to the right just before turning.

For a right turn, first check traffic behind. If it is safe to go, signal right and move to right side of lane. Continue to signal. If there is more than one lane going in your direction, move to the right of the rightmost lane. Slow down just before the crossroad, and be prepared to stop. If there are no vehicles coming the other way, or from other streets, complete your turn and then return to the left side of the road. If there is traffic coming the other way, stop, wait until the way is clear and then go.

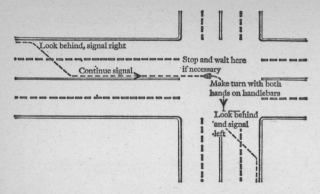

Look behind, signal right

Continue signal

Stop and wait here if necessary

Make turn with both hands on handlebars

Look behind and signal left

If, before the turn, there is a lot of traffic behind you, or the intersection is busy, or it is night-time and you have generator lights which go out when you stop, signal a stop, stop on the left and dismount, and walk your bicycle across when safe to do so.

Make signalling a habit. Always signal, even if there are no other vehicles about.

In theory, motorists and cyclists have equal right of way. In practice, many motorists feel that they have the right of way. They may be wrong, but any accident, even slight, will wind up with *you* being hurt. Fault does not matter. To survive in traffic you must take into account the fact that many motorists have never ridden a bicycle, and are unfamiliar with the problems of the cyclist.

For example, try never to block overtaking cars. But if it is unsafe for you to let them pass, don't hesitate to take full possession of your lane so that they *can't* pass. Otherwise, if you hug to the left, a motorist may be tempted to pass when there is not enough room – and run you off the road. Don't be afraid to assert your rights. You are every bit as entitled to use of the road as the motorist.

The fact that motorists are somewhat protected against injury, while you are not, means that you cannot rely on the road rules and your 'rights' for protection from accident. You must be a Defensive rider. This means always anticipating any trouble or hazards *in advance*, and not allowing yourself to be caught in emergencies or dangerous situations. A good measure of this is how often and hard you use your brakes. If you are braking a lot, you are not riding Defensively. Here are the basics of smooth, safe traffic cycling:

◎ Keep your hands on or near the brakes at all times. Traffic is not the place for no-hands riding.

◎ Be alert. Keep your eyes moving constantly. When looking behind do not twist your head, duck it down. This is quicker and smoother. Always know what kind of traffic is behind you. You might have to swerve to avoid an obstacle or serious accident and must know if you have the room or not.

◎ Be definite. Ride in a straight line. Signal all stops and turns clearly. Help other road users by letting them know exactly what you are going to do. Don't suddenly change your mind.

◎ Be defensive. Always assume the very worst. You cannot see around the stopped bus. *Assume* someone will come out from behind it hopping on a pogo stick. There is a car waiting to cross your lane ? *Assume* it will, because *it will*. This has happened to me more times than I can remember. In four out of five accidents involving bicycles and motor vehicles, the motor vehicle committed a traffic violation. Don't rely on the rules! Leave yourself enough stopping room to allow for mistakes by other people.

◎ Imagine what you might do in an emergency. Look for openings in traffic, drives, streets, garages, etc. that you can duck into should the need arise. Try to plan where you would go should you and the bicycle part company. These are things you must think about before they happen. Incidentally, the natural tendency if there is to be a collision is to try desperately to stop. Many times you are better off launching yourself over an obstacle. Far better to hit the pavement at an angle than a car head-on.

◎ Look ahead. There is a car double-parked in the next block. Are you going to have the room to swing out ? The traffic signal ahead – what colour is it likely to be when you reach it ? Anticipate traffic conditions before they occur. It is this ability that marks a skilled cyclist – or motorist.

◎ Keep moving, without exceeding a speed which allows you control. A lot of the danger from motor vehicles comes from the great difference in speed. For example, if you are moving slowly when you swing out to pass a parked car, you are exposed to overtaking traffic for a longer period of time.

◎ Keep clear. Do not follow other vehicles too closely! In most accidents, it is the bicycle which runs into something. Motorcar brakes are better than bicycle brakes. Leave enough room! It is in this situation that many motorists will press you from behind, even though you are moving at the same speed as the vehicle in front of you. The motorist following behind wants to pass and slip into the space you have allowed to give yourself enough room in which to stop. Do not let it happen. Of course once the traffic in front speeds up, allow traffic from behind to overtake.

◎ Don't weave in and out of traffic. Motorists are not expecting a bicycle to pop up. They may not know you are there, and an accident can result from this. Pedestrians crossing a road on which cars have halted also do not look out for bicycles. If you are weaving through traffic they may step out into your path. Watch especially for this when you see a bus stop.

◎ Be extra-cautious at crossroads where you already have the right of way. Vehicles coming from the opposite direction and turning right will frequently cut across your path. Even if the vehicle is waiting for you to pass, don't trust it. Letting a vehicle precede you to clear the way is often a good tactic.

◎ Another danger at crossroads is vehicles coming up alongside from behind and then making a sudden left turn. One way to stop this is for you to be in the centre of the lane. However, if the cars coming up from behind are moving fast, stay out of the way.

◎ Very often you will be riding next to parked cars. Be especially careful of motorists opening car doors in your path. Exhaust smoke from exhaust pipes and faces in rear-view mirrors are warning signals. Even if a motorist looks right at you and seems to be waiting for you to pass, give him or her a wide berth. They might still open the door in your face.

◎ Keep an eye on the road surface. Watch for broken glass, stones, pot holes, bumps, etc. If you have to hit something, get off the saddle and keep your weight on the pedals and handlebars.

◎ Look out for overtaking cars coming from the opposite direction. Many times an overtaking motorist will not notice a cyclist coming the opposite way. This is especially true if visibility is bad, or the sun is behind you.

◎ Many things can cause a bicycle to skid and fall:

— Oil on the road. This is found at the centre of traffic lanes at busy crossroads, and on sharp curves. When cars stop or turn hard, a little oil drips off.

— Newly wet streets. Roads have a light film of oil which when mixed with water makes a very slippery surface. Rain eventually washes this away, but for the first 20 or 30 minutes, be extra-cautious.

— Wet manhole covers and steel plates can dump you in a hurry. Be careful going around corners on city streets in the wet.

— Wet cobblestones are also very slippery.

— So are wet autumn leaves.

— Gravel and sand on a road are dangerous. The small particles roll on the road surface when you hit them, easily causing a skid.

⊙ Look out for storm drains. Most have the slots set diagonally to your direction of travel, but some do not. These can trap your wheel and send you flying.

⊙ The speed of traffic on clear-way streets which have no parking is usually too high to permit safe cycling. If you run in the centre of the lane, you block traffic. If you keep to the side, cars whiz by you at high speeds with only inches to spare. Stick to streets with parked cars and look out for opening doors.

⊙ Watch for cars and lorries pulling out on to the road. They may do it unexpectedly and without signalling. Always keep an eye on drives, building entrances, construction sites, taxi ranks and any other possible place that a car may come from suddenly. Remember, you are easily overlooked by many motorists. They look right at you, but they do not *see* you. Don't trust anybody. Expect the unexpected.

⊙ Pedestrians are also unreliable. They don't think 150 pounds of bicycle and rider coming towards them at 25 mph means anything, and will frequently walk right in your path. Use a bell or horn or yell – and give them the right of way if you have to.

⊙ Watch out for children. They sometimes race out suddenly into the street.

⊙ When cycling with companions, ride single file. Do not ride abreast.

⊙ If you have parcels, boxes, or other luggage, carry them on a proper rack, or in panniers or saddlebags. Do not carry with one hand or balance on the handlebars.

⊙ No passengers. Not on the handlebars, saddle or rack. The extra weight makes the bicycle difficult to control and stop.

⊙ Do not hitch rides by holding on to motor vehicles!

⊙ You are required to have lights at night. A white light at the front, and a red rear light marked BS 3648 mounted on the centre line or offside of the bicycle, not more than 20in from the rearmost point, and between 15 and 42in off the ground – in other words, where people can see it. See Chapter 9 on Accessories (pp. 83–85) for a full discussion of lights.

◉ A red reflector on the rear of the bicycle is also required.

All these rules, regulations and endless cautions are depressing. Cycling in traffic takes skill and constant attention. But you can get used to it. If you are an alert and Defensive rider, you are reasonably safe. In return for the risks, there are many benefits. But never forget: a moment's carelessness in traffic may result in an accident happening *to you*.

If you can avoid traffic, do so. It is illegal to cycle on footpaths or in most parks. However, mixing pedestrians and cyclists is a lot safer than mixing motor vehicles and cycles. Crowded pavements are to be avoided, and when you meet pedestrians give way, dismounting if necessary. But many footpaths are little used and are a far more sensible choice for the cyclist than running with the road traffic. Just remember that cycling on a footpath or in most parks makes you liable to breaking the law.

methods of dismounting from a Bicycle.

6 Accident drill

Some of the things I am going to tell you now may be
frightening. But accidents do happen. Most are minor such as a
fall resulting in a scrape or cut that needs only a wash and a
plaster. Some are serious as when you run off the road into a
tree or a lamp post, or are hit by a car. Or perhaps it happens to a
friend. You need to know what to do. Not knowing, or doing
the wrong thing, can result in still worse injury. You should
take a first aid course at your school or local hospital. I can
give you only a little information here.

After an accident *shock* is often a problem. One moment you
are rolling along, and the next instant Blam! you are down and
possibly hurt. It is surprising, and can leave you dazed and
kind of helpless . . . shocked. You may not be able to move
about very well, or you may be hurt and not feel it.

For an accident which is relatively minor, say having the
bicycle skid out from underneath you, first take stock and see
how badly you are hurt. Some people think it is brave to just
pick themselves up and keep going. There is nothing sissy about
taking care of yourself.

If you have no cuts or bruises . . . great! Check out the
bicycle to make sure it has not been damaged, that the brakes
work, wheels spin, handlebars are straight – and then go on
your way.

If you have cuts or scrapes and there is not an awful lot of
blood, go home, wash the wounds clean of dirt and grit, and put
a bandage on. If you are far from home, go to wherever you can
wash up or get help – a nearby school, hospital, doctor's surgery,
police station or private home. Again, check out your bicycle
before using it.

If you take a really nasty spill, or are hit by a car, you may be seriously injured. Try not to move about or be moved. If it is a friend who has been injured, move him or her *as little as possible*. Movement can cause further serious injury. The immediate thing is GET HELP. A passerby or friend should go immediately to the nearest phone-box, police phone, or house, dial 999, ask for the police and give the nature and location of the accident.

Keep warm. An accident victim should be gently covered with coats, sweaters, etc. If you or somebody else is on a road, be sure people are posted to warn and slow down oncoming traffic. Keep calm, and wait until help arrives. The only exception is if there is a major cut and fast bleeding. This can be very serious. Make a compress out of the cleanest cloth you can find and apply it directly to the wound. Hold it tight to stanch bleeding. If this does not help enough, and the wound is on an arm or leg, tie a strip of cloth or rope around the limb above the wound.

As you can see, the worst problem would be if you were by yourself, with no one nearby, and if you were seriously hurt. If you are cycling by yourself, make sure somebody knows where you are going, and when to expect you. Better still, cycle with a friend who can go for help if necessary.

Take care of yourself. Cuts and bruises are all part of the game. You can get them cycling, playing games or just taking a bath. But if you are out by yourself on a lonely road, take extra care, be aware that you are your only help, and try to prevent any accident from happening in the first place.

7 Touring

A bicycle is a great way to travel, but it is when you go touring that it really comes into its own. Cycling is the best way to see the country or explore a town. In a car interesting scenes and people flash by quickly. It is too much trouble to stop, turn around and go back. There are many places a car cannot go. And cars cost money. Walking is free, and you get a good, long look at the countryside, but you have to carry everything. It's hard work. A bicycle is the perfect compromise. You go fast enough to cover ground, but can see and enjoy the scenery. It is easy to stop for a close look at something interesting, or a chat with somebody. The bicycle carries your gear. It is much easier than walking. And it costs virtually nothing.

What is a bicycle tour ? This depends mostly on you. A bicycle tour can be an afternoon's jaunt to the swimming pool. It can be a weekend expedition exploring areas like the Cotswolds, Devon or Cornwall. It can be a summer's journey, covering thousands of miles. You can travel light, putting up at hostels or inns, or carry your own camping equipment, stopping where and when you please. Tours can be carefully organized and planned, with special equipment, maps, routes, etc., or they can 'follow where the road goes', as fancy takes you. Touring is pretty much a matter of style, of how you go about it.

Of course, touring is an art. There is plenty you can learn about it, and I'll try to cover all the important basic points in this chapter. But the main thing is to get out and going. One essential is a toolkit, for otherwise a breakdown may strand you many miles from home or a bicycle repair shop.

For short trips your basic toolkit should include:

A few nuts and bolts
A pump, puncture repair kit, and spare tyre valves
Tyre levers, screwdriver
Combination spanner, or 6-in adjustable spanner
Spare chain masterlink for bicycles with $\frac{1}{8}$-in chain or
Short length spare chain and chain tool for bicycles with $\frac{3}{32}$-in chain
Spare bulbs for lights.

A longer journey wants the above, plus:

Spare spokes, nipples, and a spoke wrench
Spare brake pads
Spare brake and gear cables. Trim these to proper length before
embarking or carry wire snippers.

Where to go

Start with short day trips from your home that cover no more
than 10 to 20 miles. Save the long distance and overnight
journeys until you have some experience and have built up your
strength. One idea: find your home on a map. Draw a circle
round it 10 miles in radius. Now look and see what interesting
places are within the circle. A park? A castle? Old ruins?
Farms? A lake or river? Any one should make a comfortable
day journey there and back. Do you have any relatives or friends
living nearby? If so, plan a visit.

Once you have built up your capacity and experience,
expand the circle and look for new places. When you have
reached the limit of a day's travel there and back, try an
overnight stay. A few of these and you should be prepared to
deal with a long distance, continuous tour.

Another way to go touring is to take a train to an interesting
area. This is especially good if you live in a large city. Draw a
circle on the map around your home that includes all places
within an hour's train ride. Pick a place and go. Your bicycle
will travel in the guard's van. Be sure to tie it firmly to the side
of the van so that it does not fall down and get damaged. At the
time of writing British Rail charges one-half adult fare for a
bicycle. You can fox them by reducing your bicycle to
components from which a bicycle may be assembled. Just nip down
to your friendly bicycle shop and get a large bicycle box. Find
somewhere at or near the station to keep it. When you go, just

remove the wheels and pedals, turn the handlebars around flat, and pop the lot into the box. Now your bicycle can go with you as baggage – for free. At your destination reassemble your bicycle, find someone to look after your box, and have a nice day's outing.

Ideas on where to go touring can be obtained from various organizations.

British Cycling Bureau
Great London House
Hampstead Road
London NW1 7QP

gives away leaflets on good touring areas and itineraries for a number of tours. General information is also available from

Tourist Information Centre
64 St James's St
London SW1

For the Cotswolds area there is a book, *Explore the Cotswolds by Bicycle*, by Suzanne Ebel and Doreen Imprey, available for 50p from the CTC (address below). The CTC also sells *The Roadfaring Guide to S.W. England*, 7p.

Touring on your own, or in company with a friend or two, gives valuable basic experience. But the best way to take up touring is to join the

Cyclists' Touring Club
Cotterell House
69 Meadrow
Godalming, Surrey GU7 3HS

The CTC covers all of Great Britain. It is divided into local branches called Sections, and these in turn form part of larger regional groups called District Associations. Each Section has regular programmes of cycling activities, social events and tours. Many Sections have Junior Divisions.

Riding with a Section you go on a tour which has been planned to be safe, interesting, and comfortably within your capacity. There is an experienced group leader. Most important, you get friendly help and advice from your companions – and

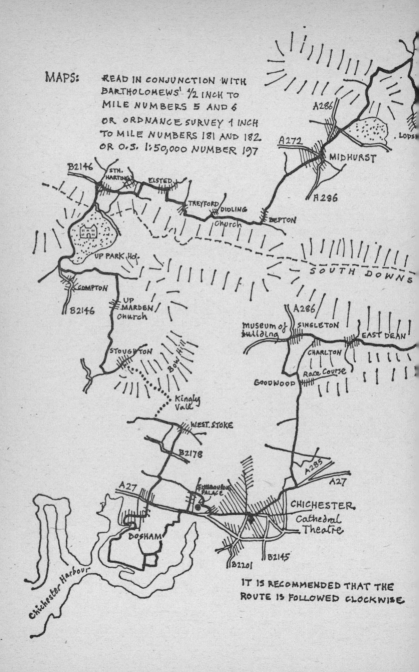

MAPS: READ IN CONJUNCTION WITH
BARTHOLOMEWS' ½ INCH TO
MILE NUMBERS 5 AND 6
OR ORDNANCE SURVEY 1 INCH
TO MILE NUMBERS 181 AND 182
OR O.S. 1:50,000 NUMBER 197

A286
LODSW.
A272
MIDHURST
A286

B2146
STH. HARTING
ELSTED
TREYFORD
DIDLING
Church
DEPTON

UP PARK Hot.

SOUTH DOWNS

COMPTON
B2146
UP MARDEN
Church

A286
Museum of
Building
SINGLETON
EAST DEAN

STOUGHTON
Bow Hill
CHARLTON
Race Course
GOODWOOD

Kingly
Vale

WEST STOKE
B2178

A285
A27

A27
FISHBOURNE
PALACE
CHICHESTER.
Cathedral
Theatre

BOSHAM

B2201
B2145

Chichester Harbour

IT IS RECOMMENDED THAT THE
ROUTE IS FOLLOWED CLOCKWISE

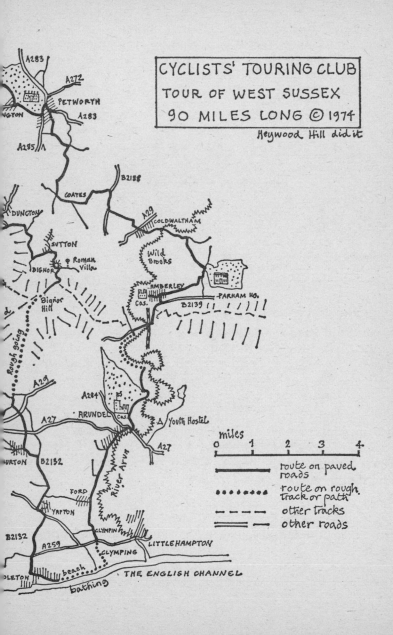

CYCLISTS' TOURING CLUB
TOUR OF WEST SUSSEX
90 MILES LONG © 1974

Heywood Hill did it

learn a lot quickly. Some people put off joining the CTC until they feel that they can 'hold their own' with other riders. Don't! Most CTC members welcome the chance to introduce people to cycle touring, and you'll learn more riding with them than in a month of Sundays if you go it alone.

The CTC also runs Organized Tours that last for two or three weeks. These include all kinds of fun activities. Just to give you an idea, here are a few that were held in 1975:

Tour No. 1 Welsh Marches Visiting Castles en route, Offa's Dyke, Severn Valley Railway, Elan Valley. For young cyclists up to age 15. Hostels and guest houses. Moderate pace. (12 days)

Tour No. 3 Canada (British Columbia) West coast of Vancouver Island to the 'Sunshine Coast' of British Columbia mainland. Routed mostly on logging roads – very suitable for cycling – including visit to Pacific Rim National Park (Canada's newest) and Strathcona Provincial Park. Travel by air. Hotels, plus one or two hostels. Very leisurely – suitable all ages. (21 days)

Tour No. 8 Southern France A fortnight in the Gorges du Tarn area. Travel by air from Ashford to Clermont-Ferrand. Fairly strenuous (50–60 miles per day). Suitable for younger age group. Hotels. (14 days)

Tour No. 9 Northants, Cotswolds and Thames Valley Specially designed for young cyclists aged 11 to 15 years. About 40–50 miles per day, with physical activities, games, swimming, etc. Accommodation in hostels. (14 days)

Tour No. 12 Lakeland Rough-Stuff Climbing most passes, especially Hard Knott, Wrynose, and Black Sail, seeing most lakes and traversing Old Coach Road, Garburn Road, and Ennerdale. Visits to Ravenglass & Eskdale Railway, Keswick Museum, and possibly including some boating. Hostels. 14–18 age group. Moderate pace. (10 days)

In addition to the Section runs and Organized Tours, the CTC has a Touring Department, which not only has available a large library of comprehensive, personally researched tours complete with maps such as the one on the previous two pages but which will also plan and suggest tours for routes and areas you request, as well as advising on equipment, maps, travel books, etc. Membership includes the Cyclists' Touring Club Handbook, jam-packed with information on places to eat or sleep, bicycle repair shops, good touring areas, equipment and plenty more. Membership also includes subscription to the bi-monthly *Cycle Touring*, filled with news of interest to the cyclist, articles on touring and tours, equipment tests, letters and general advice.

As if all this were not enough, the CTC also offers a variety of insurance services for the cyclist and his or her equipment. Membership automatically includes third party insurance up to £250,000, and in case of an accident, help and advice from the Club Legal Aid Department.

Another organization providing an accommodation handbook, touring and insurance services and maps, is

British Cycling Federation
26 Park Crescent
London WIN 4BL

Cheap accommodation is offered by the Youth Hostels Association. There are about 400 hostels in the UK, and over 4000 throughout the world. Many are in beautiful or historic areas. Accommodation is simple and inexpensive. You can bring your own sleeping bag, or hire one for a nominal charge. There is a fully-equipped kitchen, and sometimes meals or a picnic lunch can be purchased. You help with the chores.

Headquarters
YHA Trevelyan House, 8 St Stephen's Hill, St Albans, Herts AL1 2DY

Branches
YHA 29 John Adam Street, London WC2N 6JE
YHA 40 Hamilton Square, Birkenhead
YHA 36–38 Fountain Street, Manchester M2 2BE
YHA 35 Cannon Street, Birmingham B2 5EE
YHA 35 Park Place, Cardiff
YHA East Bay House, East Bay, Colchester, Essex
YHA 7 Glebe Crescent, Stirling, Stirlingshire, Scotland SK8 2AJ
YHA 39 Mountjoy Square, Dublin, Eire
YHA Bryson House, Belfast BT2 7FE

"SAY, MISTER, PLEASE TO RING YOUR BE-E-LL."

The YHA, in company with the CTC, also runs organized bicycle tours. Called Adventure Holidays, these cover moderate daily distances with plenty of time left for exploring, swimming, etc. Here are a few that were held in 1975:

Yorkshire Dales 7 days The Yorkshire Dales National Park is a wonderful holiday area with plenty of interest, marvellous scenery, rivers and waterfalls. Starting and finishing at Skipton, the tour covers a large area as far north as Keld with the last night at Linton.

Suffolk and Essex 7 days Beginning at Colchester, this holiday takes in many of the attractions of this part of East Anglia, its picturesque villages and coastline. By a circular route, visiting Castle Hedingham, Nedging Tye and Blaxhall, the holiday ends at Colchester where it began.

Devon 7 days This holiday shows you some of the best scenery Devon has to offer, combining a visit to Bellever Youth Hostel in the middle of Dartmoor with the beautiful south coast. Beginning at Steps Bridge near Exeter, your route takes you to Lownard on the edge of Dartmoor, then on to spend two nights at Salcombe, a hostel set in a semi-tropical garden. After continuing along the coast to Plymouth, you return to Steps Bridge via Bellever.

Day trips, journeys by train to interesting areas, organized tours – where and how to go depends on you. Be sure to read the section here on equipment. Rough-stuffing and camping means one kind of equipment; fast day runs with accommodation at hostels and inns, another.

Riding

When you tour take the smallest, least travelled roads possible. These are B class roads and smaller. On the big roads motor vehicles whiz along at up to 70 mph. Everything happens fast, and if something goes wrong there is little time for a cyclist or motorist to brake or manoeuvre. Accidents tend to be serious. Fewer cyclists ride in the country than in the city, but more are killed in the country. Small roads keep motor vehicle speeds down to around 30 mph, which allows more time to avoid accidents. These roads meander and take longer from one point to another, but are usually more scenic and interesting. The point of cycling is to see the countryside. If you're in a hurry, take a train. If you are forced to take an A road, or an expressway, look for an adjoining footpath.

You do not have to use roads. Bridlepaths (which cyclists are legally entitled to use) and footpaths (which they are not) honeycomb Britain. You can go for many, many miles without ever seeing a road. The scenery is usually fantastic. The riding is demanding: you may encounter mud, rocks, streams, or even snow. Best of all, there are no cars. This makes everything much more relaxing. A club specializing in this sort of touring is

The Rough-Stuff Fellowship
51 Banks Road
Linthwaite
Huddersfield, Yorks HD7 5LP

You must be 14 years old to join, however, or 10 if you join as a family member.

Safe riding on country roads is largely a matter of common

sense. Rules for traffic riding apply, and here are some other points:

◉ Always imagine 'what if?' Look and think ahead. For example, never go into a curve with a motor vehicle overtaking from behind. If a car – or lorry! – comes the other way there will not be enough room.

◉ Keep in mind how fast the cars and lorries are moving. At 70 mph they catch up with you quickly. If you crest a hill, for example, and there is no oncoming traffic, move over into the opposite lane for a while. This avoids the hazard of overtaking cars whose drivers cannot see you over the brow of the hill.

◉ Be very suspicious of other people. They do crazy things. Coming down a hill you may be doing 30 to 50 mph, a fact that many motorists and pedestrians do not understand. If you were a large lorry they would be sure to take notice. But as a cyclist, to them you are slow and unimportant and so they will stop or drive out on to the road or overtake. The idea that people can look right at you, and then act as if you are not there, may seem incredible, but it happens all the time.

◉ With the unexpected in mind, always try to have somewhere to go should everything go wrong. Where will you go if that tractor pulls out? Is there enough room for you to swerve if there is a dog behind that bush? If a car comes around the corner on your side of the road, are you going to try for a ditch or grab for a tree? You may wreck a bicycle by going off into a field, but this is a lot better than being smashed by a car. Think about these things as much as possible. Then when an emergency arises instead of panicking you may be able to take the quick action necessary to save your life.

◉ Mind your brakes. After running through puddles or wet grass dry off by applying them lightly as you ride. Going down steep hills do not hold the brakes on steadily. They can overheat and fade. Pump them on and off, and if it is a very long hill, stop once in a while and check that they are not overheating.

◉ Keep well to the left, but leave room to manoeuvre. Broken pavement, storm sewer gratings, broken glass and other odd litter can crop up unexpectedly.

◉ Look out for farm machinery. Many farmers drive on public roads as if they were in the middle of a field.

◉ Watch for loose gravel, dirt or sand, especially at driveway and side road entrances and on hair-pin bends.

◉ Bridge gratings, cattle guards, railway tracks, etc. can easily dismount you.

◉ A motorist driving into the sun may not be able to see you; be extra careful at sunrise and sunset.

◉ Dogs. Dogs can scare the wits out of a cyclist. It is terrifying to have some great beast come cannonballing out from behind a bush and start chewing on your leg.

Now, as it happens, most dogs attack according to a pattern. They circle behind the cyclist and try to pull up alongside:

So in most cases you can just step on it and outrun the dog.

Not all dogs attack according to a pattern, however. Or you may be cycling uphill and not be able to put on enough speed to outrun the dog. Relax, because the problem is not as serious as it appears. There are very few really vicious and unfriendly dogs. Most of the dogs that chase cyclists are perfectly likeable – there is just something about the sight of a cyclist that drives them crazy. So the solution to a dog attack is usually simple. You stop! Now you look 'normal', like the other people the dog knows. Often the dog will come up with tail wagging and you can make friends. When you leave, walk away and the matter will be forgotten.

If, after you stop, the dog continues to threaten to attack, stand your ground. Keep your bicycle between you and the dog. Point your finger at it, and in firm tones say 'No'. Keep calm. Most of the trouble with dogs comes because everybody gets excited. After the dog settles down a little bit, walk slowly away. Don't run – this will excite the dog again.

Every so often someone does get bitten. If it happens to you, get help *immediately*. Go to a doctor or police station, whichever is nearest. Find out who the dog belongs to. Report the incident to the police. All of your expenses, damage, etc., are the responsibility of the dog owner. In any case, see a doctor, even for a slight wound.

Technique

In touring, cadence or pace is extremely important. If you go too fast, you'll wear yourself out. Go too slow and you'll feel sluggish and tired. The ideal is a balance, a pace which gets you going but does not burn you out.

Take it easy at first. If you start out with a rush, full of zip and beans, you may strain muscles. The next day you'll hardly be able to move. Stick to the lower gears and don't push hard on the pedals. If you come to a steep, killer hill, walk up. Take it easy. That way you'll go the whole distance.

Make your rest stops short. You want to keep your body going. Stops for longer than 10 minutes cool you down and make getting started again harder.

Vary your riding position to give muscles a rest. Going into the wind, get low down. With the wind behind sit up straight and get a free push.

Always take a little food. Some sweets will do, but these do not have much food value. A better bet are the protein bars sold in health food shops. Carry something. Stores have a funny habit of being closed or far away when you are hungry.

Equipment

If you like, you can go touring on a uni-cycle. You'll find it hard work though. The best cycle for road touring is a 5- or 10-speed club sports with wide range gears. Mudguards are useful. Look at the Accessories chapter (Chapter 9) for more information.

For rough-stuff bridlepath touring a club sports, carefully ridden, will do. But if the going gets muddy and rocky, probably a standard 3-speed roadster is a better bet. Knobby 'speedway' tyres are particularly effective.

Baggage: How you load your bicycle is important. First rule: put all the baggage on the bicycle, not on you. Second rule: load evenly and low. Piling everything in one place makes the bicycle unstable.

There are three kinds of bicycle carriers: handlebar bags, saddlebags and panniers. If you are travelling light a saddlebag will do. These fasten to the seat post and can carry a lot of gear. The next addition would be a handlebar bag. This distributes weight fore and aft, and the bag is handy for items needed immediately, such as food, cameras and rain gear. Get one with a transparent map case. For long journeys and camping trips, fit rear panniers. These hang on special frames alongside the rear wheel and have plenty of carrying capacity.

Karrimore makes an excellent line of cycling and camping luggage equipment available at most bicycle shops. The YHA stores also sell this sort of equipment.

When you load, put heavy items on the bottom, light fluffy things on top. Keep items like rain capes and tools within easy reach. Give yourself a few trial runs; the extra weight changes the way the bicycle handles and takes getting used to.

Maps and compass: A compass is not only useful when used in conjunction with a map, but can itself guide you in the general direction you want to go. This is especially handy on cross-country jaunts. Stand away from the bicycle when you take a compass reading, as the metal of the bicycle may affect the compass.

Maps are, of course, vital if you wish to follow a particular route. But the other advantage of maps is that, with them, you

Runaway!

can stay *off* main roads and *out* of dull, uninteresting areas.

Petrol station maps are not detailed enough. The Ordnance Survey Maps are excellent and obtainable in many bookshops. These are extremely detailed, showing individual buildings, walls, tiny streams, hostels, inns, old ruins, etc., and are wonderful for close exploring of an area. For overall route planning $\frac{1}{2}$in scale maps are the best. Bartholomew's $\frac{1}{2}$in series is obtainable in bookshops and, together with the Ordnance maps, from the CTC at a reduced price for members.

Sometimes it is fun to forget about the map and just go where fancy takes you. Ask directions as you go. People can tell you of interesting routes, scenic attractions, swimming places and the like. But have a map in reserve!

Clothing: Cycling is warm work and you do not need much in the way of clothes. Shorts are fine – morning chill disappears after two or three miles. Make sure yours are comfortable in the crotch. For your top half several thin garments which can be put on or taken off as needed are better than one bulky coat. A T-shirt, ordinary shirt and windcheater are usually enough. Perhaps a light sweater if the weather is cold, or to wear in the evenings. Cycling shirts have handy large pockets. Whatever you wear, go for bright colours that help to make you visible to motorists. For rain protection, a cycling cape and sou'wester hat. Rain suits give better protection but make you all sweaty. Use shoes with a firm sole, not sneakers or tennis shoes. These do not give enough support to the foot.

Tip: if you become chilly, slip a few sheets of newspaper under your jacket or shirt to cut out the wind.

Camping: Cycle camping is great fun, and inexpensive. It allows you to go when and where you please.

Camping sites are not difficult to find. If you ask politely, and promise to make a neat camp with no garbage left behind, most people will give permission to camp on private land. They may even see you off with hot doughnuts in the morning! There are also many camp sites. A list is available from

British Tourist Authority
239 Old Marylebone Road
London NW1

Organizations are useful. Membership in

The Camping Club of Great Britain and Ireland
11 Lower Grosvenor Place
London SW1

gives you an International Camping Carnet, insurance services,
a handbook on camping, and a guide to 1500 sites in Great
Britain and Ireland. Another organization is

Cycling Section
Association of Cycling and Lightweight Campers
30 Napier Road
Wembley, Middlesex

Equipment: How you go camping and the kind of equipment you use is a matter of personal choice. Some people lug along all the comforts of home – stoves, lanterns, tents, radios, record players and the like. Others make do with a poncho and a blanket. If you are unfamiliar with the craft of camping, get a good book on the subject. There is room here only for generalized suggestions.

1 Sleeping bag. Your most important item of equipment. For warm weather use, inexpensive bags filled with synthetics such as 'Dacron 88' and 'Astrofil' are adequate. For colder weather and high altitudes, the more expensive down filled bags are the best. For maximum range and comfort, get one that is multi-layered and that will take a flannel insert.

2 Waterproof ground sheet, such as a poncho. This can be improvised into a tent.

3 Mattress. An air mattress is comfortable to sleep on but bulky. A thin ensolite pad is fine.

4 Tent. Good for protection against rain and bugs, and for privacy. I prefer to travel light and improvise shelter as needed.

5 Cooking gear. Fires are prohibited in many areas, and wood is scarce in others. Lightweight alcohol, paraffin, and gas stoves are quick to set up and use. A mess kit of nested aluminium pots, pans, plates and cups is very handy, but aluminium is toxic. I prefer a small steel frying pan and a small steel pot and to eat from them direct. Skewers can be used to

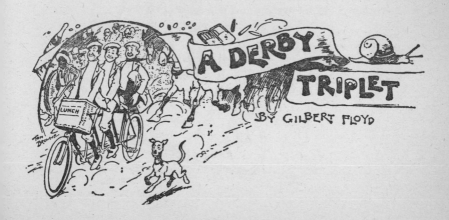

A DERBY TRIPLET
BY GILBERT FLOYD

cook food, make a grill to support a pot or pan or peg down a tent, and they are very light.

6 Food. Always take a little along with you. You might suddenly want to stop miles from a store, or find the store closed. Do your shopping in the afternoon. A mixture of dried fruit, nuts, cereals, sugar and dried milk is nourishing and easy to carry in plastic bags. Eat it as it is or just add water. Always have a canteen or drinking flask of water. There might not be any water where you choose to camp.

7 Lanterns. Bulky and cumbersome. A small flashlight is sufficient. Go to bed early and get up with the sun.

8 Bicycle games and racing

Bicycle games

Bicycle games are fun and help develop riding skill. The
number and kind of games you can play is limited only by your
imagination. There's only one rule – don't play on roads
where motor vehicles run. Best places are playgrounds, empty
parking lots, courtyards, fields and parks.

Follow-the-leader

One person sets off and the rest of the group follows in a single
file. Each cyclist must follow exactly in the path of the leader,
who tries to shake off the following cyclists by riding the
trickiest possible course. Anybody who veers off the course is
out. Followers who manage to stick with the leader for a
pre-arranged length of time – say five minutes – are winners.
If the leader shakes off all the followers within the time limit,
then the leader is the winner.

Tag

For this game you need some weak string that you can easily
break with the hands. Tie a 12- or 15-foot length of string to the
rear mudguard of each bicycle. Tie a bit of wastepaper to the
free end of the string, so that it trails out behind when the
bicycle is ridden.

Set boundaries. Anybody who rides outside is *out*. One
person is *it*, and tries to catch the string of one of the other
players with a foot or a wheel. Once somebody is *tagged*, they
are *it*.

Remember to use string for this game. Bicycle tag with direct contact is likely to involve collisions and accidents.

Hide-and-seek

For this game two objects about twenty feet apart are needed. These can be anything – a couple of jackets on the ground, two trees, two park benches, etc. One is *home*, the other is *call*. One player is *it* and stands at *call* with eyes shut, counting to 100 while the other players scatter and hide. At the count of 100 *it* opens eyes and starts looking for the hidden players. When *it* spots a player, *it* must ride back to *call* and shout out the name and location of the player. If a player reaches *home* without being *called*, he is *home free*. If a player is *called*, he is *out*.

Slalom

For this you need a watch with a sweep second hand, and some empty cardboard boxes or other markers. Arrange the boxes to form a course with curves and short straight stretches. Time each rider through the course. Touching the ground with feet is not allowed. The rider with the shortest time is the winner.

Stop

Two riders coast towards a line at the same speed. At the line they brake and try to stop in the shortest possible distance. Winner then takes on the next contestant, and this process is repeated until each member of the group has had a go. Winner of the last *stop* is the group winner.

Pursuit

For this game you need to mark out a race course. Two riders start, one from the start line, the other from half-way around the course. Each rider tries to catch the other.

Straight-line

Find two parallel lines on the pavement, or mark them with water-soluble paint. Who can ride fastest down the lane without crossing the lines? The slowest?

Race

Mark out whatever kind of course you like. It can be smooth and fast, or include tricky sections with obstacles like mud, hills too steep to ride up, fences which must be climbed over or even a stream to ford! To avoid collisions and tangles it is best to time each rider separately over the course, or to run a series of elimination heats with two or three riders per race.

Racing

Cycle racing is an international sport. If you like hard, demanding, strenuous competition, then it may be for you. It will keep you very fit. To compete, you must be 14 or older, and join one or even two organizations, depending on the type of event(s) in which you compete. These organizations are listed at the end of the chapter. At first you will race against beginners like yourself. Wins will promote you in grade so that you are always competing against other riders of similar ability and experience.

There are basically four types of events: time trial, road race, track and cyclo-cross.

Time trial

Each rider is either timed separately over 10, 25, 30, 50 and 100 mile courses, or rides as far as possible in 12 or 24 hours. Each competitor rides alone, and must pace himself to achieve the shortest possible time.

Road race

Everybody starts together, first rider over the finish line wins. Single-day races are between 50 and 100 miles. Stage races are run over a number of days and can cover great distances. The Tour de France, for example, is about 2600 miles. In road racing riders are pitted against each other. Strategy is very important. One rider may follow another, letting the fellow in front do the hard work of breaking the wind, and then sprint for a win at the finish. Teams work together to block opposition riders and keep a strong team mate out ahead. In big races like the Tour de France bicycles collide and pedals jam into spokes.

There are accidents and riders are hurt. This is one reason, in fact, why the time trial type of event was developed – to prevent accidents.

Track

Track races are run on oval, banked courses. The machines used are ultra-light, with no gears or brakes. Speeds are high – up to 60 mph.

Cyclo-cross

Cross-country races from point to point or around a course, from 1 to 16 miles in length. The typical course includes steep climbs and descents, plenty of mud, thick woods, streams and even hurdles. It is a rough sport, with plenty of spills.

Speedway

A grass-roots sport as yet unrecognized by any 'official' organization, these are races run on dirt track ovals using stripped down bicycles with low gearing and studded track tyres. Fast action, with lots of broadside skids and spills.

Conditioning

As I've said, racing is a demanding sport. If you compete seriously you will have to train and keep fit with a year-round conditioning programme. There isn't enough space to go into details of this sort of thing here. Get advice from your club, or from your school athletic department.

Equipment

A lot of people invest large amounts of money in fancy racing machinery. Unless you are competing in very advanced events, the important thing is the rider. A basic club sports will do you perfectly well to start.

To race, you will need to belong to one or even two organizations, depending on the type of event(s) in which you compete. Here are the addresses of the national organizations:

Maurice Cumberworth (General Secretary)
British Professional Cycle Racing Association
Hebden Travel Lodge
Mill Lane
Hebden, Yorkshire
(Pro racing under BCF rules)

W. F. Gill (Secretary)
Cycle Speedway Council
67 St Francis Way
Chadwell St Mary
Grays, Essex RM16 4RB

British Cycling Federation
26 Park Crescent
London W1
(International, affiliated to Union Cycliste Internationale)

R. J. Richards (General Secretary)
British Cyclo-Cross Association
5 Copstone Drive
Dorridge, Solihull
Warwickshire

E. G. Kings (Secretary)
Road Time Trials Association
210 Devonshire Hill Lane
London N17 7NR

Irish Cycling Federation
155 Shanliss Road
Shantry
Dublin 9, Eire
(Also known as the CRE, supervises organized cycle racing in
Irish Republic. Many races are held under the National Cycling
Association, which is not internationally recognized.)

J. E. Fletcher (Secretary)
Northern Ireland Cycling Federation
144 Princes Way
Portadown
County Armagh
Northern Ireland
(Ulster sport, but the NCA operates here also)

The appropriate national organization above will supply you
with the name and address of a local club for you to join. Time-
trialists need only be a member of a club affiliated to the Road
Time Trials Council, but competitors in other events must also
take out membership with the British Cycling Federation
(address above).

9 Accessories

A lot of people are tempted to load down their bicycles with accessories. This just adds excess weight and results in harder pedalling. Use only those accessories you really need. This depends on the kind of bicycle you have, and what sort of cycling you do. There is little point in outfitting a hi-riser to go touring, or stripping a roadster to go racing.

Bicycle pump: Every bicycle should have one. As there are three different types of tyre valve (see p. 122), be sure your pump fits the type you have.

Mudguards: These add greatly to comfort in wet conditions, and all but flat-out racing bicycles should have them. Plastic mudguards are light, and easy to get on and off. Stainless steel and aluminium are stronger, and offer mounting points for lights.

Lights: Lights are not so much for you to see by, as for you to be seen. It is both dangerous and illegal to ride at night without lights, white at the front and 'BS 3648' marked red at the rear. There are two types of lighting system: battery or generator. Each has advantages and disadvantages.

Generator lights are powered by a hub dynamo or by a spring dynamo which rides against the wheel. Generator lights stay consistently bright and cost less to run than battery lights. They are bolted on to the bicycle, discouraging pilferage, but permanently increasing weight. The dynamo creates drag when you ride, and when you stop the lights go out. If you need to ride very slowly up a steep hill or along a rough track, there may not be enough speed to keep the lights bright. Generator lights require wires which can snag on branches or other objects and break.

Battery lights eventually fade, particularly when used continuously for a long period of time. They can be removed from the bicycle to save weight on daytime rides, or to serve

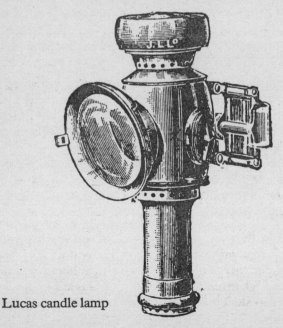

Lucas candle lamp

as a flashlight for night camps. They do not go out when you stop – good not only for safety, but also for map reading or roadside repairs at night.

In general, for people who need lights infrequently, the battery type is the best choice. If you opt for generator lights, and ride mostly at night, use a hub dynamo. It has less drag than a spring dynamo. The spring dynamo has the advantage however, of dragging only when in use, and is the better type if your need for lights is not great.

Many long-distance tourists use generator lights as a main system, and a battery light for camp use, map reading, and emergency light in case the main system fails.

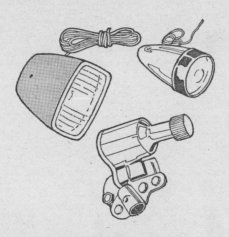

Whatever type of system you use, carry spare bulbs. Room to store these can often be found inside the lamp, or you can wrap them in a bit of plastic and stuff them in the ends of the handlebars.

Horn or bell: These just add weight. Plain yelling is quicker, more reliable and more expressive.

Carrier: The best sort of carrier depends on your needs. A cloth rucksack can go with you on and off the bicycle and is handy for shopping. For carrying the odd parcel or schoolbag, a light aluminium rack fitted over the rear wheel is sufficient. For heavy loads, a steel rack designed for use with panniers is best.

See p. 69 for more information.

Lock: See pp. 31–32.

Toe clips: Used on club sports bicycles, these are a metal cage and strap to hold your foot on the pedal. They greatly increase pedalling efficiency, and as long as you ride with smooth-soled shoes (not sneakers or shoes with soft rubber soles), your feet can be slipped out easily in an emergency.

Bicycle shoes and cleats: Bicycle shoes have a steel shank to provide strong support for the foot. They are essential for racing and a great boon for the long-distance tourist. Cleats are

BLUEMEL'S SPIRAL TROUSER CLIP

metal or plastic grooves nailed on to the soles of bicycle shoes. Used together with toe clips, they firmly affix the feet to the pedals, and are suitable only for racers or experienced long-distance tourists.

Rear view mirror: A bicycle wiggles about too much for a rear view mirror to be reliable.

Water bottle: Useful on very long tours and races.

Flint catchers: For use with tubular racing tyres only, these are curved bits of wire which ride just above the tyre and brush off broken glass, pebbles, etc.

Kickstand: A matter of personal preference. There is usually something handy to lean the bicycle against, and I prefer to eliminate the extra weight.

Chainguard: These are useful for preventing oil stains from brushing your leg on the chain, but are too much extra weight on a club sports or racing bicycle. With pants, always use trouser clips, or tuck the cuff into your sock.

Odometer: Tells how far you have gone. I don't think knowing this is important.

Speedometer: No bicycle speedometer is accurate. If you want to know your speed, time yourself over a measured course.

Helmet: Vital. Three-quarters of the serious injuries in cycling accidents are to the head. Protect yours. Use a helmet for road and track races, and for riding in traffic. The conventional cycling helmet, made of padded leather straps, is not good enough. Use a hard shell helmet. For warm weather use, drill some holes in the helmet for ventilation.

10 Cyclepaths

Cycling is a nice way to get about. But it could be much easier and safer. At present most roads are made primarily to serve motor vehicles, and cycling on them is dangerous. Separate cycles and motor vehicles and the problem is solved. This is done by constructing *cyclepaths*, which are separate roads for bicycles only, and marking *cycle lanes* for bicycles only on existing streets and roads. Once bicycles and motor vehicles are separated, cycling becomes more safe . . . and enjoyable.

There are some towns in England where this has been done. Stevenage, in Hertfordshire, is an example. Stevenage has separate roads for motor vehicles, bicycles and mopeds, and pedestrians. Where different roads meet, under- or over-passes are used to avoid intersections. As a result there is not a single stop sign, traffic light or pedestrian crossing in the entire town. You can walk or cycle anywhere you want without ever encountering a motor vehicle. Motorists are also well served by this system, because they never have to stop for an intersection, pedestrian or cyclist. The average speed of motor vehicles in Stevenage is 20 mph, about double the average in other towns. So the system is convenient for everybody – pedestrians, cyclists and motorists alike.

More important, it is safe. In twenty years there have been only about twenty cycling accidents in Stevenage. These were minor, with little injury or damage. The general accident rate in Stevenage is half the national average. In fact, Stevenage reckons that it saves £28,000 a year in hospital expenses on account of the safety of its transportation system. Still more money is saved because there is no need for traffic police or wardens, or traffic lights.

Stevenage is a New Town, built just after World War II. Because the builders started from scratch, and used common sense and imagination, they were able to create a transport system which takes everybody's needs into account. What about a town which is already built ? It may not be so easy to install cyclepaths. What can be done to provide for cyclists ? The answer is – plenty. On streets and roads special *cycle lanes* can be marked and set aside for cyclists. Motor vehicles are banned from these lanes. Streets that have little motor vehicle traffic can be made into *cycle routes*, on which bicycles have priority over motor vehicles. *Cycle trails* can be made through parks, countryside and forest, making use of bridlepaths, disused railway tracks, and footpaths.

The use of footpaths is worth special mention. As a general rule cyclists are forbidden to use footpaths. This is supposed to be for the safety of pedestrians. However, in Stevenage cyclists and pedestrians have freely shared the footpaths without incident for twenty years. There is little danger in mixing the two; both cyclist and pedestrian are exposed and vulnerable, and both take pains to avoid accidents. Cyclists were banned from footpaths in England in the mid-1930s. At the time, motor vehicles were fewer in number and travelled at slower speeds, so that cycling on the roads was much safer than today. Now there are many more motor vehicles and they move at very high speeds, making cycling on the same roads dangerous. The risk of accident in mixing pedestrians and cyclists is very much less than in mixing motor vehicles and cyclists. (Of course, when and if you do ride on footpaths, have consideration for pedestrians. Dismount and walk if the path is crowded.)

Cycle lanes, cycle routes, cycle trails, and the use of footpaths and parks are provisions for the cyclist that can be made immediately. But best of all are proper cyclepaths, entirely separate from other roads. Did you know that a cyclepath benefits not only the cyclist but the community at large? A 12-foot wide cyclepath can carry five times as many people as a 24-foot wide motor vehicle road, yet costs only one-sixth the per-square-yard cost of the road! And cyclists don't create noise or air pollution. The energy in one gallon of petrol,

40 miles

1500 miles

How far they would go on the energy from 1 gallon of petrol

which will drive a motor car 20 to 50 miles, will, consumed as food, drive a cyclist 1500 miles!

Here are some things you can do to help bring cyclepaths to your area: Write to your local and county authorities and ask them what they are doing to encourage cycling. Point out the advantages of bicycle transportation. Tell them the cost of a cyclepath in comparison with a motor vehicle road. What about parking for cycles? On the street, sixteen bicycles will fit into the same space as one car. In a car park garage, 220 square feet is used (including aisles) for each car. *Thirty* bicycles could be parked in the same space. Ask if they know that the Organization for Economic Co-operation and Development reports that motor vehicle bans increased business in shopping areas of Vienna by 25–50 per cent, in Norwich by 15–35 per cent, and in Rouen by 10–15 per cent.

Write to your local newspapers. Complain about the lack of provisions for cyclists. Write about the advantages of bicycles.

Here is a perfect school classroom project: design a cycleways system for your area.

Get a large map. Mark on it any existing facilities for cyclists. Now mark all the schools, factories, offices, shops, parks and places of interest that need to be served by a cycleway. Work out routes from residential areas to these places which are as direct as possible, going along back streets, footpaths, bridlepaths, disused railway tracks, etc., and which need the minimum of construction. Some conflict with existing roads is unavoidable, and will be resolved with traffic lights, bridges or underpasses when the plan is accepted. Your routes should also provide for recreational cycling and access to the surrounding countryside. Cycle the routes yourself. Note where parking should be provided and what major problems, if any, exist. Plot all of the routes and information on your map. You can get help and advice for this project from

All Change to Bikes
Greater London House
Hampstead Road
London NW1 7QP
Tel: 01–387 0116

Once you have completed your plan/proposal, enlist as much support as possible. Present the plan for comment to school, health, hospital and traffic authorities. Then send copies of the plan, together with letters of support, to your local authority, asking for their comments, to All Change to Bikes, and to your local newspapers. If you have done a thorough job, you'll get action.

If you don't, organize a bicycle demonstration. Print up posters announcing a rally in support of cyclists. Say that you have got a solid, workable plan to provide for cyclists' needs that will also benefit the entire community and that you want your plan put into effect! Put the posters up all over town, and especially in schools and in cycle shops. Notify the newspapers and radio and TV stations. Send them copies of the plan. On Rally Day have a short ride around town together, and then go as a group to your local authority and present them with copies of your plan. Demand a date by which they will make a public comment on the plan.

Always make a positive approach. You and your friends are trying to win public support and sympathy. Be well informed on the advantages of bicycles, not only for yourselves but for everybody else. Cyclepaths mean fewer injuries, fewer obstructions for motorists, saved hospital expenses, etc, etc.

In order to gain attention one of you might choose to exercise civil disobedience, and be arrested for cycling on a footpath or in a park. The ensuing trial provides a chance to dramatize the plight of cyclists. It shows that you are serious. But consider carefully: the point of civil disobedience is to break the law, and you are thus liable to fine or even jail.

Discuss the possibility of civil disobedience with your parents and teachers, and make your own decision about doing it.

Such an extreme course of action is not likely to be necessary for you. The case for cyclepaths is a good one. Most people respond warmly to the idea of cyclepaths and understand that they benefit the entire community. What they need is help in knowing where and how to build cyclepaths. And giving this help is what you can do.

TESTIMONIAL.

To Messrs. HILLMAN, HERBERT & COOPER, LTD.

Ghostland, December, 1889.

Dear Sirs,—I left the old world through an accident, the result of a fall from a so-called safety bicycle by one of the too numerous jerry makers, who, being without the means to build cycles with limbs of steel, resort to the fatal practice of casting in large pieces.

My present object in writing to you is to express my unbounded gratitude for the "Premier" cycle you made for me. It carries my weight well, and although the roads are full of clinkers and other rough products of combustion, the grade of steel of which it is composed is so fine, and its temper so excellent, that the 5,000,000 miles I have traversed upon it have not impaired it to any appreciable extent.

In contrast to this I have seen machines brought here by ill-advised Ghosts, which I will simply describe as *not* "*Premiers*," made of such common soft material that they have melted like butter in the sun.

You will be somewhat astonished at the number of miles I have ridden in this land, but the fact is that one has to take a deal of exercise to keep one's form as a Ghost, and I prefer to take all mine on a "Premier." Besides, a Ghost has to be in many places at one time, and that means fast travelling.

I congratulate you on that wonderful ride on a "Catford Premier" safety by Holbein!!! **324 miles at one go!!!** If ever that man comes to these parts, where the physical conditions are so different to those you are familiar with, and gets down to the weight of a healthy Ghost, he will do about 1,000 miles a day.

I have learnt with great satisfaction that you have made more cycles than any other maker during the past season; that your factories are the largest, and your machinery the finest in the world. I should wonder how your rivals find purchasers were it not for the fact that I know all cyclists are not able to get your wonderful machines, the supply, great as it is, being limited.

I enclose my photo, taken by an old gentleman in these parts who has only just commenced the photographic art. The likeness is not a very good one; you may therefore not recognise the features of,

Yours very truly,

JOHN NOTELEKS.

FOR LISTS APPLY TO

Hillman, Herbert & Cooper, Ltd.

PREMIER WORKS, COVENTRY.

London Office & Depot: 14, Holborn Viaduct, and 5, Lisle St., Leicester Square.

11 Maintenance and repair

Contents

General

When you have got a bicycle you will want to keep it in tip-top condition, right ? Not necessarily. Some people just want a knockabout, rough-use machine. They don't care if it gets dirty and rusty. Their idea of maintenance is to wait until something breaks, take the bicycle to a shop and say 'fix it'. Other people make a career of polishing their machines. They are forever adjusting, disassembling, lubricating or replacing some part.

What you do is up to you. What I can tell you is that if you don't maintain your bicycle sooner or later it will break, usually at a very inconvenient time and place.

Out of track.

The point of maintenance is to prevent breakdowns. Secondly, a well lubricated and adjusted bicycle is much more fun to ride. So, after a while, maintenance becomes a joy rather than a chore. This is especially true for performance bicycles, such as club sports models.

You may not be very interested in maintenance, in which case I hope you have a simple bicycle, such as a single- or three-speed roadster. I recommend that you take it to a cycle shop for servicing at least twice a year. A bicycle is a machine. It will eventually break down if it is not serviced.

So that you know what I am talking about, here is a diagram of a bicycle with all the parts labelled:

S—PBB—C

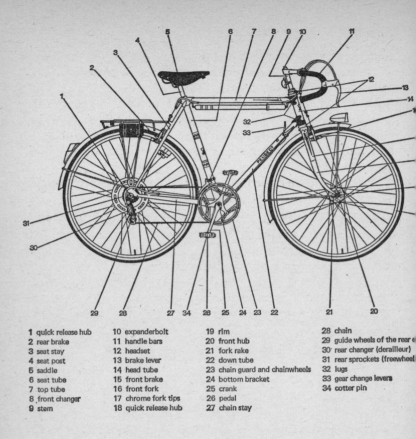

1 quick release hub	**10** expanderbolt	**19** rim	**28** chain
2 rear brake	**11** handle bars	**20** front hub	**29** guide wheels of the rear c
3 seat stay	**12** headset	**21** fork rake	**30** rear changer (derailleur)
4 seat post	**13** brake lever	**22** down tube	**31** rear sprockets (freewheel
5 saddle	**14** head tube	**23** chain guard and chainwheels	**32** lugs
6 seat tube	**15** front brake	**24** bottom bracket	**33** gear change levers
7 top tube	**16** front fork	**25** crank	**34** cotter pin
8 front changer	**17** chrome fork tips	**26** pedal	
9 stem	**18** quick release hub	**27** chain stay	

We'll now discuss the various kinds of maintenance a bicycle
needs. At the end there will be a chart giving a rough timetable
for these operations.

Cleaning

Keep your bicycle clean. Dirt is abrasive. It works into the
moving parts and makes them wear out faster. Once a week go
over the entire bicycle with a soft cloth. Use an old toothbrush
to clean out the nooks and crannies. Protect the paint finish
and chrome parts with automobile paste wax or LPS-1 spray
every six to nine months. Do not wax or spray the wheel rims
where the brake shoes make contact.

Lubrication

A bicycle has hundreds of moving parts. Lubrication is vital. However, the type and amount of lubricant is important. Too little, and parts which rub against each other will be dry and wear out quickly. But too much lubricant forms a gooey mess which attracts dirt. The result is an abrasive mixture which also speeds up wear. The rule is: keep the bicycle clean, and lubricate it regularly but sparingly. A little lubricant will go a long way.

There are three basic types of lubricant. Each has specific uses:

1 LPS. This is a lubricant and rust preventative developed for use on aircraft. It comes in spray cans in three grades of thickness (LPS-1, LPS-2, LPS-3), and as a paste (LPS-100) which may be used as a grease. The great advantage of LPS is that it dries clean, so that it does not attract dirt. It also displaces water, and cannot be washed away. LPS is more expensive than oil or grease, but works very well, and is quick to apply.

2 Oil. The standby. Do not use household oils such as 'Three-in-One'. These have a vegetable gum base which ultimately creates a hard residue – the last thing you want! Use a proper cycle oil, such as Sturmey-Archer, or motorist's SAE 30 oil, which is the most economical. Oil can be used for almost all the parts of the bicycle, including the hubs, pedals, chain, gear changing mechanisms, brakes, cables and, sometimes, the bottom bracket.

3 Grease. Obtainable from cycle shops, or auto accessory shops. Grease is used for bearings:

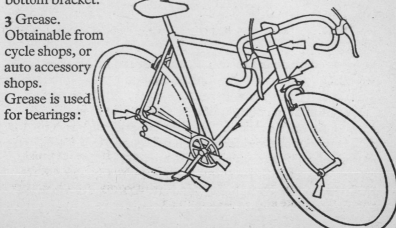

Chain roller, wheel hub and pedal bearings usually need dismantling and regreasing every six months; headset and bottom bracket bearings every twelve months. These jobs are tricky and require special tools. In most cases they are best left to a cycle shop. If you want to do the work yourself, then get *Richard's Bicycle Book* for full instructions.

Some bearings are both greased and oiled. You can tell these by the fact that there is an oil cap or clip:

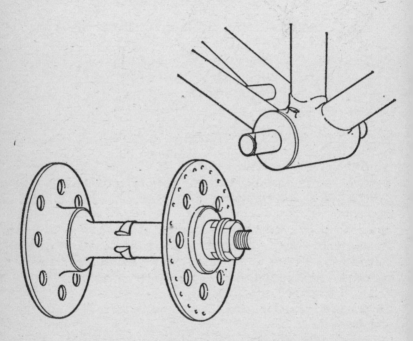

These need oil once a month. A multi-speed internal gear hub between one and two teaspoonfuls, a coaster brake hub between one and two tablespoonfuls and a regular hub about half a teaspoonful. Some bottom brackets are set up to use oil. A teaspoonful once a month. Too little is better than too much. If oil leaks out of the sides of the bearings and dribbles all over your crankset or wheels, you are using too much.

I prefer the use of LPS spray for the chain, freewheel, derailleur, brake pivots, cables and any other parts which do not use grease:

The spray is easy to apply with pinpoint accuracy, displaces water, and dries clean. This is really important. The trouble with oil is that it attracts dirt. In the case of the chain, for example, this means that every one or two months you have to remove it, soak it in paraffin or other solvent and then oil and install. It's time-consuming and messy. If you use LPS, you need do this job only once every three or four months, depending on how much you use your bicycle. Since the spray goes on in seconds, you can lubricate the chain every two weeks. Same for the freewheel and derailleur. LPS is particularly useful for the brake pivots and all cables. Oil has a tendency to leak out on to the brake levers and handlebars and brake shoes. Once a month is sufficient.

Special note: oil evaporates. New bicycles fresh from a dealer and bicycles that have been unused for a long time may be dry. Be sure to lubricate before using.

Tools

You can get by with very little in the way of tools. A tyre repair kit with levers, a dog-bone combination wrench, a 6- or 8-in adjustable spanner, and a $\frac{1}{4}$-in tip screwdriver are all you need to start with. Later on, when you tackle more difficult maintenance jobs, you will need some of the tools listed below.

A good way to reduce cost is to share one set of tools with several friends.

For both 3- and 10-speed bicycles:

From an ironmonger's	*From a cycle shop*
⅛-in tip screwdriver	Raleigh all-purpose wrench
pliers	hub wrenches
wire clippers	spoke wrench
hammer	
6-in mill bastard file	

For 10-speed bicycles, *from a cycle shop*
chain tool
allen wrenches, metric
freewheel remover
There are two kinds of
freewheel remover:

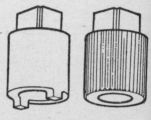

Look at your freewheel and find out if it is splined or not on the interior to see what kind you need.

If you have a Campagnolo derailleur, a Campagnolo combination allen and socket wrench. If you have cotterless cranks, a crank removing tool.

Working on your bicycle is easier if you can hang it up off the ground. Rope strung from a tree limb or building rafter will do.

General words

1 This chapter covers the basics of lubrication and adjustment. There is not enough room to deal with more involved work, such as dismantling bearings or derailleurs. For a complete manual, see *Richard's Bicycle Book*.

2 Plan and organize your work. Ripping helter-skelter into a job usually results in a maze of disassembled parts which you are unable to fit back together. First read about and consider what you are going to do. Make sure you have all the necessary tools. Then, while working, lay out parts in the order in which they came apart. Put tiny parts in boxes, jars or egg cartons. Take the time to be neat and organized – it will speed the work considerably.

3 Work within your limitations. In gardening there are those people who have a 'green thumb', a natural ability to help things grow. Similarly, some people have a natural bent for working with machines, while others do not. If you don't have at least some fun and satisfaction from doing your own work, I suggest you leave it to a cycle shop.

4 You may find a part on your bicycle which is a little different from those described here. To figure it out, find the part in this book which is most nearly similar, and then analyse the differences.

5 Do not use a great deal of force when assembling or disassembling parts. Bicycle components are frequently made of alloys for light weight. They are not as strong as steel and it is not hard to strip threads or otherwise damage parts. Always be sure that things fit. Be careful, delicate and sensitive. Fix bolts, nuts and screws firmly, not with all your might.

6 Most parts tighten clockwise and come apart turning anti-clockwise. This is called a right-hand thread. A left-hand thread tightens anti-clockwise and loosens clockwise. Left-hand threads are not used often.

7 When fitting together threaded parts, hold them together as perfectly aligned as you can, and turn one backwards (loosen) until you hear and feel a slight click. Then reverse and tighten. If this is new to you, practise on a nut and bolt until you have the feel of it perfectly.

If you get stuck with a rust-frozen nut or bolt, soak it in LPS-1 or penetrating oil, give it a few light taps to help the lubricant work in, and then try to undo it with a tool that fits exactly. If this fails, try a cold chisel and hammer:

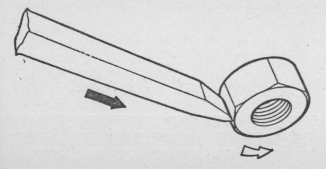

Go carefully, as if you slip you may gouge a chunk out of your bicycle. If hammer and chisel fail, hacksaw or file the nut or bolt off. How did it get this rusty in the first place?

8 There are a number of tiny little nuts and bolts on your bicycle for cable clamps, racks, brake lever mounts, gear shift lever mounts and so on. These tend to work loose and need tightening about once a month.

9 The left side of the bicycle is as if you and the bicycle both point forward.

10 Solvents: paraffin and paint thinner are good. Petrol is VERY DANGEROUS.

Brakes

Lubrication

Once a month apply a drop or two of oil or LPS to the brake yoke pivot points (centre-pulls) or the pivot bolts (side-pulls), and to the brake levers. Once every three months oil or LPS the brake cables, and once every six months grease them. Once a year remove the entire brake mechanism, clean with solvent, lubricate and reassemble.

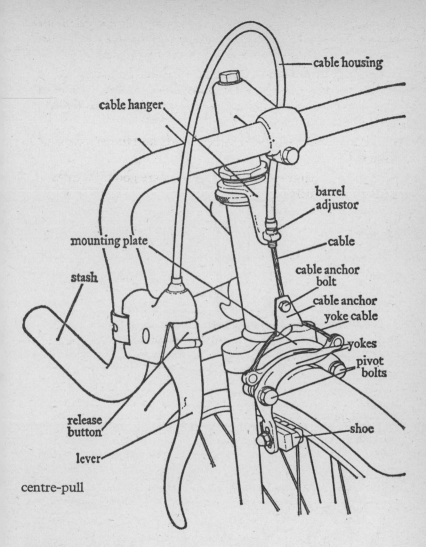

cable housing

cable hanger

barrel
adjustor

cable

cable anchor
bolt

mounting plate

cable anchor
yoke cable

stash

yokes

pivot
bolts

release
button

shoe

lever

centre-pull

Calliper brakes
Adjustment

Once a week check that the brake levers move only a short
distance before the brakes engage. If the lever comes near or
touches the handlebar, take up slack with the *barrel adjuster*.
On a side-pull brake this is almost always found on the yoke

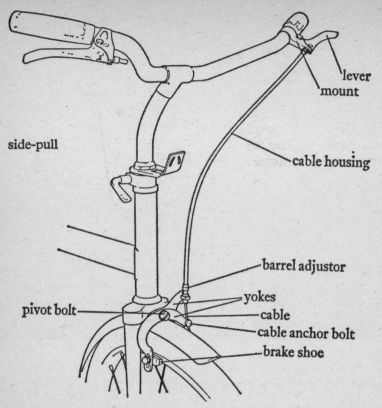

side-pull

lever
mount

cable housing

barrel adjustor

pivot bolt

yokes
cable
cable anchor bolt
brake shoe

(A), while on a centre-pull brake it is usually at the brake lever
(B) or the cable hanger (C):

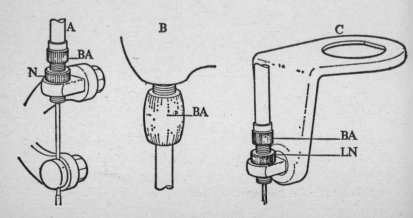

Undo the locknut LN, and turn the barrel adjuster BA anti-clockwise until you have taken up the slack.

Your barrel adjuster may have reached the limit of its travel. You must readjust the cable anchor bolt. First undo the locknut LN, and turn the barrel adjuster BA clockwise fully home:

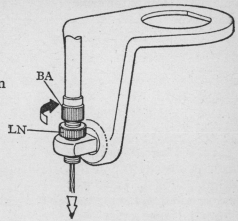

Next, you need to take the spring tension off the brakes, otherwise the cable will pass through the cable anchor bolt when you loosen it. There are a number of ways to do this. The brake yoke arms can be compressed with a tool called a 'third hand' or some string.

Most centre-pull systems have a built-in means for creating slack. This can be a small button which allows the brake lever to open more:

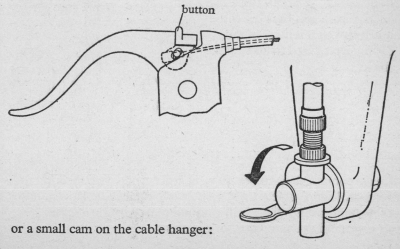

or a small cam on the cable hanger:

There should now be enough slack in the cable to lift the yoke cable YC clear of the cable anchor A:

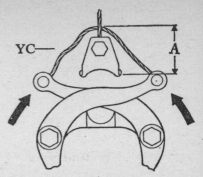

On a side-pull system the cable is slacked by first compressing the brake yoke arms, and then freeing the cable from the brake lever:

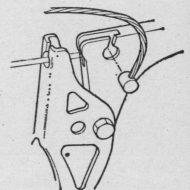

The rest of the job is now quite simple. Slacken the cable anchor bolt, and pass the cable down through it most of the distance required to take up the slack:

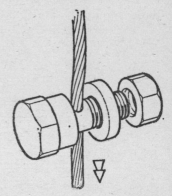

Leave enough slack to permit reassembly, e.g. reconnecting the yoke cable and cable anchor (centre-pulls), or brake lever and cable (side-pulls). Make a fine adjustment with the barrel adjuster and you are ready for the races.

Once a week check that the brake shoes are aligned so that the shoe hits the rim squarely:

Wrong   Wrong   Right

Brake shoes are held on either by a conventional bolt:

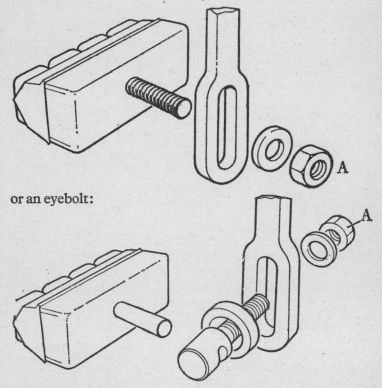

or an eyebolt:

In either case, loosen nut A, adjust brake shoe to meet the rim and tighten. One method is to loosen nut A just a little bit and gently tap the shoe into position. With conventional bolts you'll find that the brake shoe twists to the right when you tighten the nut back down. Set it slightly anti-clockwise so that the final tightening brings it perfectly into position. Do not use too much force. Brake bolt screws strip easily.

New brake shoes will frequently wear into correct alignment with a few days' use:

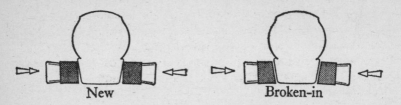

New   Broken-in

To replace a brake shoe, slide the old one out and the new one in:

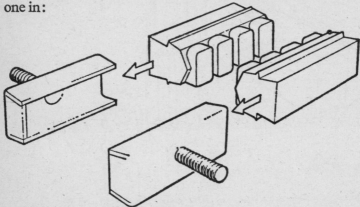

If the old one won't come out, forget it and buy another holder. Be sure to install new units so that the closed end faces forward or else the shoes will slide out when the brakes are applied.

Cable replacement

Once a month check the brake cables for wear. Any obvious defect, such as a frayed cable:

calls for immediate replacement, as does stickiness in the motion of the cable through the cable housing. It is good practice to replace both brake cables at the same time. If one has run its course, it is likely that the other has also. The inconvenience of a broken cable is not worth the gain of a month's extra use.

Unless you can specify the brand and model of brake, take your bicycle or old cable to the shop when purchasing replacement cable. Cables come in different shapes, lengths and thicknesses. It is very irritating to discover in the middle of the job that you have got the wrong part.

One kind of side-pull brake does not use a cable anchor bolt. Instead, the cable end has a ball or nipple which slips into a slot on the brake.
Both the cable and the housing must be replaced as a single unit. Compress the brake yoke arms, and release ball or nipple from yoke:

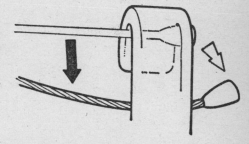

For the rear brake, loosen the clamps on the frame, and draw the unit through.

All other calliper brake units use a cable anchor bolt. Undo this (see pp. 107–8). For the front brake, slide the housing off the cable. For the rear brake, leave the cable attached to the frame, and draw out the cable. Detach the cable from the brake lever:

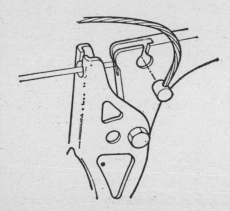

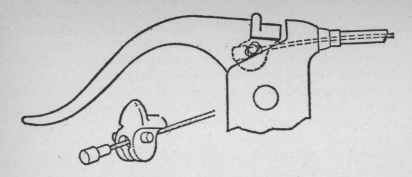

Examine the cable housings to see if they also need replacement. Are they kinked or broken?

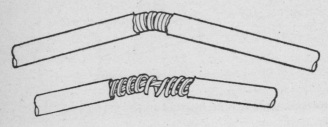

Are the ends free from burrs?

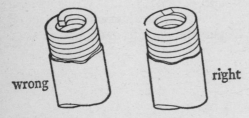

wrong   right

You can eliminate a burr by

1 Snipping off the cable housing end with a strong pair of wire cutters (pliers are not good enough);

2 clamping the cable housing end in a vice and filing it down; or

3 by using a tool called a taper ream, which you insert in the cable housing end and twist until the burr is gone.

If you use wire cutters, be sure to get the cutting edges between the coils of the housing or else you will mash the ends flat:

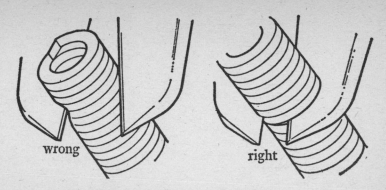

wrong   right

When installing the new cable, save any cutting for last. Cutting invariably frays the cable end and makes it hard to slide through the housing and cable anchor bolt. Installation is the reverse of removal, and for clarification look at the illustrations in that section. Grease the cable before installing.

One-nipple cable: Slip cable through brake lever mount and attach to the brake lever. Front brakes: slip housing on to cable. Rear brakes: slide cable into housing. Twist the cable or housing as you do this to avoid catching the cable:

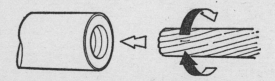

and be sure to do it in the right direction or the cable will unravel. Push free cable end through cable hanger (centre-pulls), or through barrel adjuster at yoke (side-pulls), and then through the cable anchor bolt hole. To adjust, see pp. 105–9.

Two-nipple cable (one-piece housing and cable): Attach to brake lever. For rear brakes, slide housing through clamps on frame. Front and rear, pass cable end through barrel adjuster on brake yoke arm and fix to opposite brake yoke arm by slipping ball or nipple into slot. Take up slack with barrel adjuster. Rear brakes, tighten housing clamps on frame, and take care that they are set so clothing will not snag on the screws when riding.

Brake levers
Outside bolt type

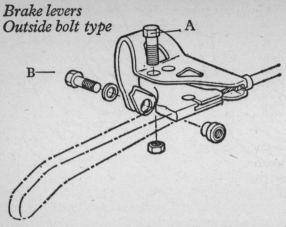

Adjust brake lever with bolt A. To adjust position, slacken B and move mount. To dismount, take off bolt B. Mount may have to be slid back off handlebar in which case grip must be removed. If your brake lever mount has a slot in the bottom:

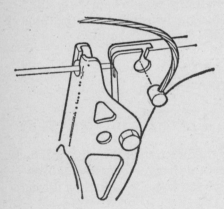

or if the cable ball or nipple will pass through the hole in the mount, create enough slack in the cable by screwing home the barrel adjuster and clamping together the brake shoes, and disconnect the cable from the lever. If this is not possible, disconnect the cable anchor bolt at the brake mechanism and take the cable out altogether.

Inside bolt type

Disconnect the yoke from the
cable anchor. Fully depress
the brake lever and use a screwdriver or socket wrench on bolt
A. If you are replacing the
brake lever, you may need to
take out the brake cable (see
pp. 110–13). On some systems,
such as the Weinmann, the
cable end will pass through the
hole B in the brake mount.

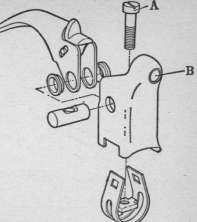

Pivot bolt adjustment/dismounting brake

Once a month check that the mounting bolt A is secure:

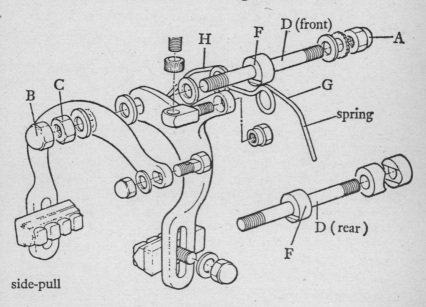

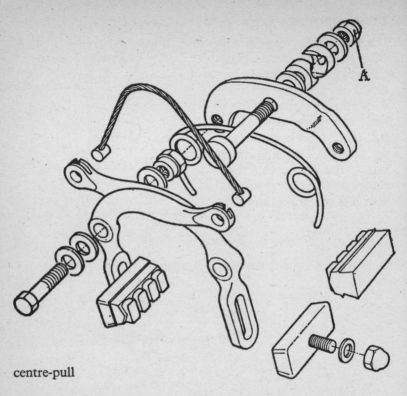

centre-pull

It is this nut A which allows you to remove the entire brake mechanism from the bicycle.

On side-pull brakes, check the pivot bolt adjustment once a month. Hold the locknut C with a wrench, and with another wrench undo acorn adjusting nut B one-half turn. Turn both C and B flush against brake yoke arm. Back off B one-half turn, hold in place with a wrench, and lock locknut C against it.

Pivot bolt adjustment for centre-pull brakes is covered under Repair, pp. 120–22.

Once a year remove the entire brake mechanism, dismantle, clean in solvent, lubricate, and re-assemble. Keep the parts in order and don't lose any – all are essential!

Roller lever brakes

As with calliper brakes, roller lever brake shoes must be aligned to hit the inside of the rim squarely. This is done by means of a metal guide (A) clamped to the fork blade or chainstay:

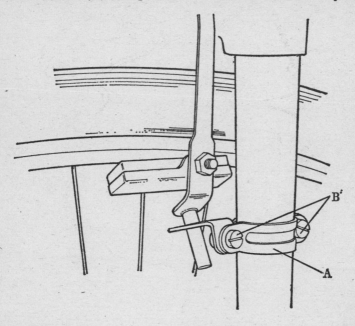

Loosen bolt B, and move guide as necessary so that when the brakes are applied, the shoes hit the inside of the rim.

If there is too much slack in the system, take it up at a connecting bolt by loosening bolt B: sliding the rods together, and then resecuring bolt B. Another way is to take up the slack with the adjusting bolt:

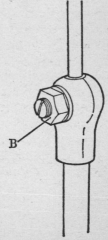

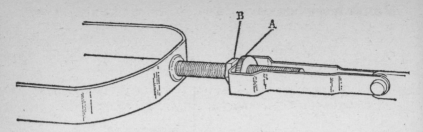

by first undoing locknut B, and then tightening nut A.

Repair

1 If brakes are weak, or do not work at all –
◉ Is rim oily?
◉ Are shoes hitting rim?
◉ Can you move brake mechanism by hand? No, see 3, below.
Yes and (a) lever moves easily, then the cable is broken. Replace.
(b) Lever is frozen, disconnect cable at brake lever end and
see if it will slide. If not, the cable is frozen. Replace. If it slides,
the lever is frozen. Adjust as per pp. 114–15.

2 Brakes judder. This is usually a loose mechanism. Adjust as
per pp. 115–16.

3 Brakes drag.

side-pulls

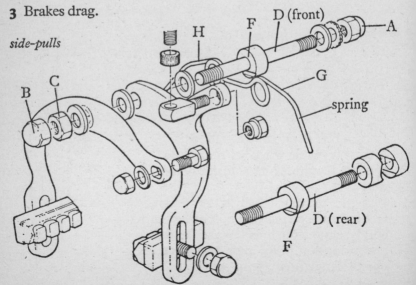

Loosen mounting bolt A, realign brakes, and tighten. Doesn't work? Examine brake seating pad F. If it has a slot for the spring, the spring must be bent. Prise it off the brake yoke and bend outwards with a pliers, on the same side that it drags. Still doesn't work?

Check to see that the brake yokes are not rubbing against each other. If so, bend them apart with a screwdriver:

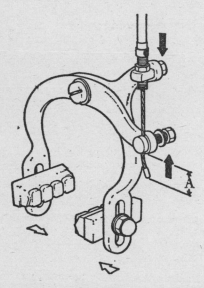

or slide a piece of fine emery cloth or sandpaper in between the yokes and file them down.

If this is not the problem and you have tried everything else, a complete disassembly (see pp. 118–22) is necessary. Study each part to see if it needs replacing (like a washer bent out of shape). It may be that the yokes cannot rotate on the pivot bolt. File down and polish the bolt, or enlarge the holes in the yokes with a taper ream or emery cloth wrapped around a nail. If none of these things work, get a new brake mechanism.

Centre-pulls

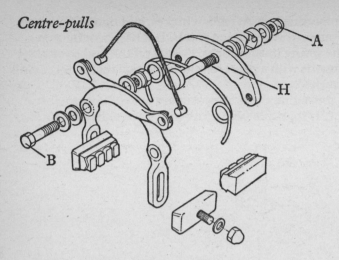

Is the cable adjusted correctly?

Are all parts there? Is the spring intact and properly mounted?

Is mounting nut A tight?

If one shoe is dragging against rim, slack off A, centre brake mechanism, and retighten A.

If both shoes stick, try lubricating the pivot bolts B while wiggling the yokes back and forth. No? You will have to disassemble the pivot bolts.

First disconnect the spring. Study the bolts to see if they are type 1, where the pivot bolt screws into the brake arm bridge H; type 2, where the pivot bolt screws into a post which comes off the brake arm bridge and on which the yoke rotates; or type 3, where the pivot bolt simply goes through the brake arm bridge and the yoke rotates on a bushing.

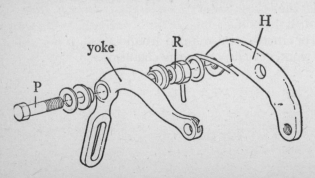

Type 1: First try slacking off the locknut R and undoing the pivot bolt P one quarter to one half turn. On some models the locknut R is on the other side of the brake arm bridge H. If the yoke will now pivot, retighten locknut R. If not, remove pivot bolt P altogether. Keep track of all the washers. Is the pivot bolt P straight? Look for dirt or scarred surfaces on the pivot bolt P and inside the yoke. Clean and polish. If yoke will not turn freely on pivot bolt, enlarge yoke hole with a taper file or ream, drill, or emery cloth wrapped around a nail. Or file down the pivot bolt. Lubricate and reassemble.

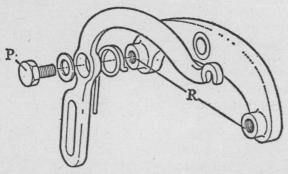

Type 2: Undo spring and remove pivot bolt P. Remove yoke and keep track of the washers. Check for grit and clean. Is post R scarred? Polish with fine sandpaper or steel wool until yoke will rotate freely on it. Or enlarge the yoke hole with a taper ream, drill, or emery cloth wrapped around a nail. Lubricate and reassemble.

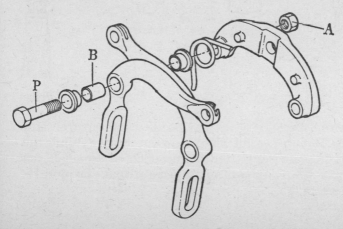

Type 3: Undo nut A and remove pivot bolt P. Keep track of bushings and washers. Is the pivot bolt straight? Is bushing B in good condition? Check for grit and clean. If yoke still sticks, try polishing pivot bolt with steel wool. Lubricate and reassemble.

Tyres

Once a week check the air pressure in your tyres. Keep them hard. Soft tyres drag when you ride, making pedalling more difficult, and they are more easily damaged.

Tubular 27in – Rear, 85 to 100; front, 75–90
Wire-on 27in – 75 to 90
Wire-on 26in × 1¼in – 45 to 60
　　　　　 × 1½in – 40 to 55
　　　　　 × 1⅜in – 40 to 55
　　　　　 × 1¾in – 35 to 45
Wire-on 24in 　　　 – 35 to 45
　　　　20in 　　　 – 45 to 50
　　　　18in 　　　 – 35 to 45
　　　　16in 　　　 – 30 to 40
　　　　12in 　　　 – 30 to 40

There are three types of tyre valve:

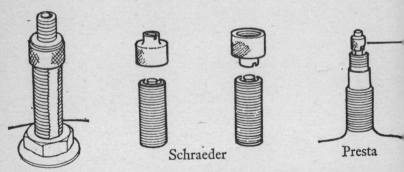

Schraeder　　　　　　　　　　　Presta

Tyres with Schraeder valves may be filled with a petrol station air pump. Be very careful not to blow out the tyre. While the required pressure is high, the volume of air is very small. Jab the air hose down on the valve for just a second – no more! – then release and test.

With a bicycle pump, ensure that the hose fitting is for the type of valve you have. Check connections periodically as you pump. With a 'Presta' valve, undo locknut A, push pump on valve, hold it firmly to the tyre with one hand, and pump with the other. When finished, disengage the pump with a sharp downward knock of the hand; wiggling it off will lose air and possibly bend the valve.

Tubular tyres breathe air out of the sides and must be checked every day. Oil and grease rot rubber; keep these away from your tyres.

When you do your weekly pressure check, look the tyres over for cuts and breaks, and clean out any stones or glass embedded in the casing.

Repair

Most tyre problems can be prevented. Once in a long while you may have a blow-out, where the tube breaks like a burst balloon and the tyre goes flat suddenly. More often you will have a puncture, a small pin-hole in the tube which leaks air slowly. These are caused by small pieces of glass or sharp stones which stick to the tyre and work their way into the casing as you ride. So watch out for these hazards. Mind where you go. If you

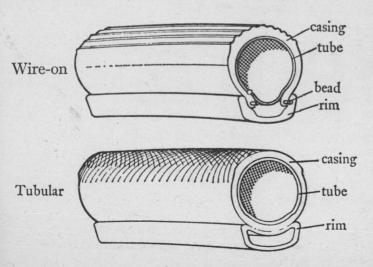

are forced to ride through a patch of broken glass, check and see that the tyres have not picked any up. Going over stones, through pot-holes, and on and off kerbs will cause ruptures in the tyre casing. Don't do these things.

To mend a puncture you need tyre levers, and a kit containing patches, glue, abrasive, and chalk. First, check the valve by inflating tyre and placing a drop of spit on the end of the valve stem. A leaky valve will bubble or spit back. Tighten the valve, and if this does not fix it, replace it.

If the valve is OK, spin the wheel and look for an obvious cause like an embedded nail or piece of glass. Yes? Dig it out and mark the spot. You'll be able to mend the puncture without removing the wheel.

If you cannot find the puncture from the outside, remove the wheel (pp. 128–31). Deflate tyre and remove the valve stem locknut. Work the tyre back and forth with your hands to get the bead free of the rim. If the tyre is a loose fit on the rim, you may be able to get it off with your hands. This is best, because tyre irons may pinch the tube and cause more punctures. To do this make sure that the bead is free of the rim all the way around. Take a healthy grip on the tyre with both hands and pull it up and off-centre so that one bead comes over the rim:

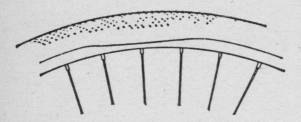

then go around the rim working the bead completely off.

You will probably need to use tyre irons (not screwdrivers, as these are likely to cut the tube). Free bead from rim. Insert tyre iron under bead, being careful not to pinch the tube, and lever it over the side:

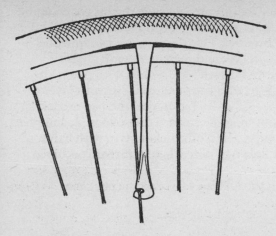

Insert the second iron a few inches away from the first iron, and past where the bead is over the rim. Lever iron. For most tyres this will do the job. No? A third iron. If this doesn't work, use the now free second iron for a fourth attempt:

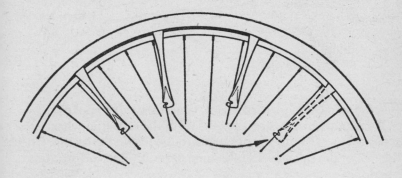

and repeat this process as often as necessary.

If you don't have tyre irons which hook on to the spokes, you will have to use elbows, knees, etc., to hold down the irons as you work away. Be careful not to crush a spoke, and keep your face clear in case something slips and tyre irons start jumping about.

When one bead is off the rim, push the valve stem up into the tyre, and remove tube. Use chalk to make a note of which way the tube was in the tyre. Inflate tube and rotate it past your ear. If you can locate the puncture through the hiss of escaping air, mark it with chalk. If not, immerse the tube in water and look for escaping air bubbles. Dry the tube with a rag while holding finger over puncture and then mark with chalk.

Take sandpaper or metal abrader supplied with patch kit and rough up the area around the puncture. Spread a layer of cement over this area and let dry tacky. Peel the paper backing off a patch without touching the surface thus exposed, and press it firmly on the puncture. Hold tube next to tyre with valve stem alongside valve hole and note where puncture occurred. Set tube aside to dry.

If puncture was on the inside of the tube, probably a protruding spoke caused it:

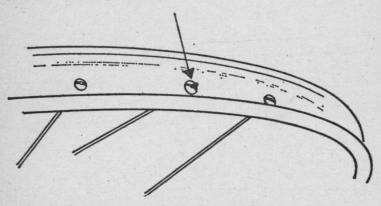

File the spoke flush with the rim. Check the other spokes.

If the puncture was on the outside of the tube find what caused it by rubbing your fingers around inside the casing. Check the rest of the casing for embedded particles, and for ruptures or breaks.

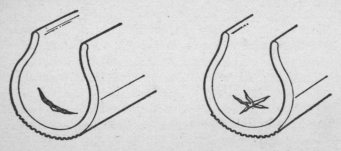

Replace the tyre at the first opportunity if it has these.

To install the tube, first inflate it slightly to prevent it from folding and pinching itself. Push the part of the tube with the valve stem into the tyre, and the valve stem through its hole on the rim. Fit valve stem locknut loosely. Stuff rest of tube into tyre, being careful not to pinch or tear it. Check that valve stem is still straight.

Push valve stem part way out, and slip bead of tyre at that point back over the rim. It is important that you hold the base of the valve stem clear of the rim as you do this, or the bead may catch on it and create a bulge in the tyre:

Work around the rim, replacing the bead and always taking care not to pinch the tube. Ideally you can do the entire job with your hands. Check that the valve stem is still straight. The last bit will be hard. Just working at it with your thumbs, first from one side, then from the other. When about 2in of bead remains give it the grand effort. Don't wonder if it will go over; decide that it will. If you have to use a tyre iron, be careful not to pinch the tube.

Wheels and hubs
(1) Wheels

Once a week check that your rims are true. Hold a pencil (or other object) braced on a stay or brake with the end almost touching the rim and spin the wheel slowly. If the rim moves away from the end of the pencil more than $\frac{1}{2}$in, it must be trued. This is done by adjusting the spokes and is a delicate job requiring patience and skill. Remove the wheel and take it to a cycle shop.

Wheel removal

Wheels need to be removed often, for a variety of reasons, and sometimes on the road. So you can and will do this with a free-standing bike, but it is much easier if the wheels are off the ground. Most 3-speeds and some 10-speeds can simply be turned upside down on handlebars and seat, as long as cables or shift selectors are not damaged. Bikes with calliper brakes in proper adjustment should require some slacking of the brakes (see p. 107) so that the tyre will pass between the brake shoes.

Front wheel, any bike

The wheel will be held to the fork by hex nuts,

wing nuts, or a quick-release lever:

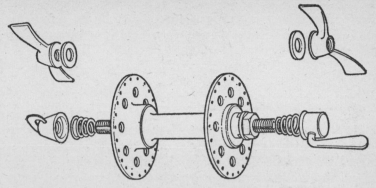

For nuts, undo both simultaneously (anti-clockwise) and unwind a turn or two. Levers, flip it. Remove wheel. Note that the washers go outside the fork drop-outs.

Rear wheel

10-speed bikes: Run the chain to the small sprocket on the freewheel. Undo nuts or lever and push wheel down and out. If you have a free hand, hold back the derailleur so that the freewheel clears it easily, otherwise just gently wiggle it by.

3-speed bikes: Shift to third gear (H). Disconnect shift cable at rear hub by undoing locknut A and unscrewing adjuster sleeve B from pole:

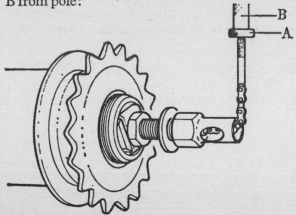

Undo nuts simultaneously (anti-clockwise). Remove wheel. Note that washers are outside drop-outs.

Single-speed coaster-brake bikes: Disconnect the coaster-brake bracket from the chain stay (metal arm at left end of rear axle), undo nuts (anti-clockwise) and remove wheel.

Replacing wheels
Front wheel, any bike

Axle with nuts: Back off the nuts a few turns and slip axle on to drop-outs. Washers go outside the drop-outs. Set the nuts finger tight and check that the rim is centred between the fork arms before snugging them down. Re-set brakes if necessary.

Levers: Slip axle on to drop-outs with the lever on the left side of the bike. If this is difficult, hold knurled cone with one hand and unwind lever a couple of turns with the other. Slip axle on to drop-outs and wind lever down just short of finger tight. Check that wheel rim is centred between fork arms, and close lever so that it points to the rear of the bicycle. It should be firmly shut. Re-set brakes.

Rear wheels

10-speed bikes: Work axle into drop-outs, slipping chain over the smallest sprocket on freewheel. Set nuts or lever for light tension. Pull wheel towards rear of bike until right end of axle hits the back of the drop-out. Use this as a pivot point to centre the rim between the chain stays, and tighten nuts or lever. Re-set brakes.

3- and 1-speed bikes: Work axle into drop-outs, slipping chain over sprocket. Lightly tighten nuts (washers go outside drop-outs) and pull back wheel so that the chain has ½in play up and down:

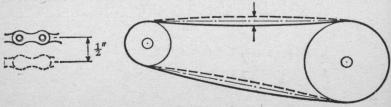

Centre rim between chain stays and fix down the nuts. Check chain tension. One-speed bikes: reconnect coaster brake bracket to frame. Three-speed bikes: with gear selector in 3rd (H), reconnect barrel sleeve to hub gear chain, and set locknut with cable slightly slack. Test gears and adjust if necessary (pp. 146–48).

Wheels and hubs
(2) Hubs Lubrication

Any front hub or 10-speed rear hub with oil clips or caps: scant ½ teaspoonful a month. If a grease fitting, one or two shots of grease a month. Multi-speed rear hubs: between one and two teaspoonfuls oil a month. Coaster brake hubs: one to two tablespoonfuls oil, or two to three shots grease, a month. Use only cycle oil or motorists' SAE 30 oil. Once a year have the hubs dismantled and re-greased.

Adjustment

Once a month check wheel bearing adjustment. If the wheel can be wiggled from side to side (usually accompanied by a clicking noise) when held at the tyre, or if the wheel will not turn easily, it needs adjustment. Wheels held with nuts or lever nuts can be adjusted while on the bicycle. Just loosen the nuts. Wheels with quick-release hubs must be removed. You will need special thin hub wrenches (cycle shops). Undo locknut A from cone B:

C is back here.

Holding axle or housing (quick-releases) still with wrench at locknut C (ten-speed rear wheels: if you can't get it with a wrench use vice-grips or pliers), screw cone B fully home and then back off one quarter turn. Lock in place with locknut A. Test for side to side play, and that the wheel spins freely.

On a three-speed hub this adjustment is made on the side opposite the hub gear chain and sprocket:

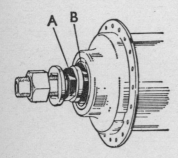

Loosen locknut A, turn cone B fully home, back off one quarter turn, reset locknut A.

On a Sturmey-Archer SC coaster hub:

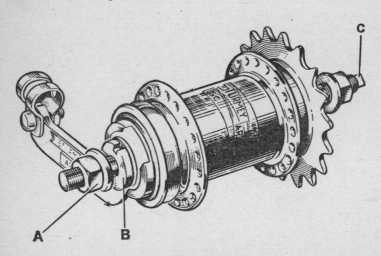

loosen locknut B, then turn C clockwise to tighten, anti-clockwise to loosen. Re-set locknut B.

Front wheel 'dynohubs' are adjusted at the left side, away from the dynamo:

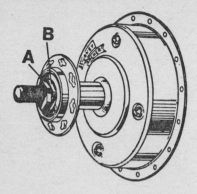

While rear 'dynohubs' are adjusted at the left side next to the dynamo:

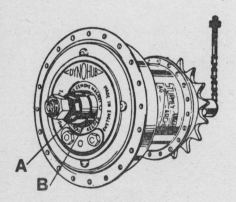

In both cases loosen locknut A, turn slotted washer B fully home, back off one quarter turn, and re-set locknut A.

Headset

The headset connects the front forks to the head tube of the frame. Once a month check the headset adjustment by locking the front brake and rocking the bicycle forward and backward. If there is a clicking noise and it is not coming from the brake mechanism, the headset needs adjustment. Loosen the locknut A:

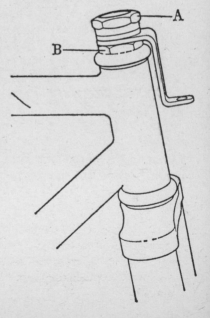

Sometimes this locknut is designed with notches. Loosen with a hammer and centre punch or screwdriver:

If you are using big wrenches or pliers, be careful not to bend nuts or races. Turn the threaded top race B hand tight against the bearings, and then back off one quarter turn. Snug down locknut A, being careful to keep threaded top race B in position. Check adjustment again.

Have the headset dismantled and regreased once a year.

Pedals

If pedal is difficult to spin, or can be wiggled back and forth on the spindle, it needs adjustment. Remove dustcap A (prise off with a screwdriver if it is the wedge type):

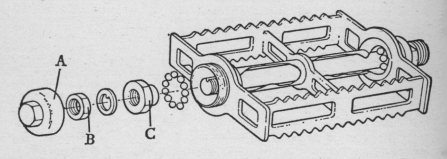

Undo locknut B from cone C. Screw cone C fully home and back off one-quarter turn. Secure with locknut A. Check for play and that pedal spins easily. Replace dustcap A.

Have the pedals dismantled and regreased once every six months.

Cranks

There are three types of cranks: one-piece; cottered three-piece and cotterless three-piece:

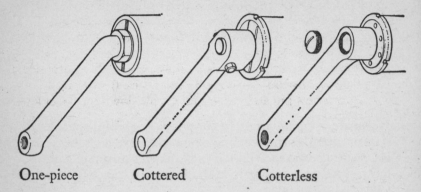

One-piece   Cottered   Cotterless

Since one-piece cranks include the bottom bracket axle, they are covered under Bottom Brackets, p. 138. To test the cranks for tightness, position the pedals so that each is the same distance from the ground. Press firmly on both pedals with hands and release. Rotate crankset one-half turn and press pedals again. If something gives, one of the cranks is loose.

Adjustment and removal
Cottered cranks

Support the crank with a block of wood which has a hole or V-notch into which the cotter pin A fits:

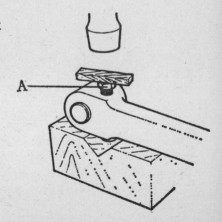

Be sure that the support block touches only the crank and is firmly in place. Otherwise what you do next will damage your bearings by driving the balls into the sides of the cup and scoring it. Next: if you are tightening, give the head of the cotter pin A two or three blows with a wooden mallet or hammer and wooden block combination. Then snug down the nut firmly, but not with all your might or you will strip it. If you are removing, undo the nut two or three turns and then tap threaded end of cotter pin. Repeat if necessary. Be careful not to damage the threads as you will want to use the pin again. If you use a new pin and it does not fit, file down the flat side until it does.

Cotterless cranks

You will need a crank installer and extractor which fits your particular brand of crank. Cotterless cranks are made of alloy, which is softer than steel, and must be handled with care. To tighten or loosen, first remove the dustcover A:

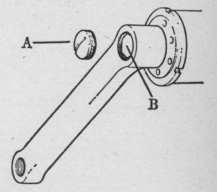

To tighten, apply socket wrench of installer to nut B and turn down, wiggling crank arm to make sure it is seated all the way home. For new cranks retighten every 25 miles for the first 200 miles of use.

To remove, first get the chain out of way. Remove nut B. Back inner bolt of extractor A all the way out:

Screw the extractor into the crank, and tighten down inner bolt A. *Do not do this with all your might or you may strip the threads.* Just tighten firmly. Now give the extractor two or three taps with a hammer, and tighten it one-eighth of a turn. Repeat until crank comes free.

Bottom bracket

One-piece crankset

If axle is hard to turn, or slips from side to side in bottom bracket shell, first remove chain. Then loosen locknut A by turning it clockwise:

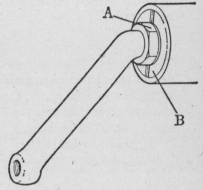

Use a screwdriver in slot of cone B to turn it fully home (anti-clockwise), and then back it off one-eighth turn. Resecure locknut A (anti-clockwise) and check that cranks spin freely without side to side play.

Three-piece crankset

To adjust, first disconnect chain. Loosen notched lockring C on left side of bracket with a 'C' wrench (bike shops) or a hammer and screwdriver combination (anti-clockwise):

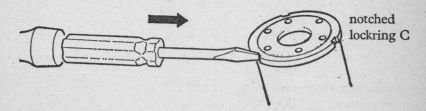

notched
lockring C

Then tighten (clockwise) adjustable cup D fully home with a screwdriver or centre-punch inserted in hole or slot and *very light* hammer taps:

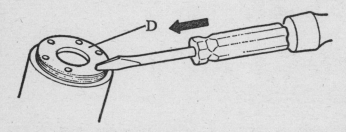

Reverse one eighth turn and secure with lockring C. Check that axle spins freely and has no side to side play. Have the bottom bracket dismantled and regreased once a year. More often if your bike is frequently out in rain or mud.

Chain

There are two kinds of chain. One is used on non-derailleur bikes, is $\frac{1}{8}$-in wide, and held together with a master link:

which can be taken apart without special tools; the other, for derailleur-equipped bikes, is $\frac{3}{32}$in wide, and has no master link (it would catch in the rear gear cluster), so that a special chain riveting tool is needed to take it apart or put it together:

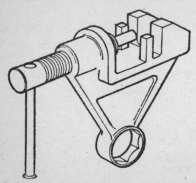

Removal and replacement

Chains should be replaced every two years on bikes that see constant service, and every three years on bikes that see average service. Although the chain may look perfectly sound, the tiny bit of wear on each rivet and plate adds up to a considerable alteration in size. A worn chain will chip sprocket teeth. On a derailleur bike, the freewheel sprockets must be replaced at the same time as a new chain is fitted.

To test a chain for wear, remove chain (see below) and lay on a table with rollers parallel to surface. Hold chain with both hands about 5in apart. Push hands together, and then pull apart. If you can feel slack, replace the chain.

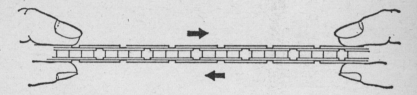

Test also for side to side deflection. It should not be more than 1in:

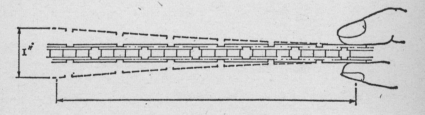

A simple test for chain wear is to try and lift one link away from the chainwheel. If it goes high enough so that you can see the top of a gear tooth, the chain is finished.

To remove and replace a master link chain find the master link and prise the lock clip off with a screwdriver:

To remove a derailleur chain drive out a rivet with a chain tool:

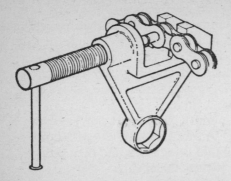

Be sure that the point of the chain tool centres exactly on the rivet. *Do not drive the rivet all the way out.* Go only as far as the outside plate. Stop frequently to check progress. Once the rivet is near outside chain plate, free link by inserting a thin screwdriver and twisting gently:

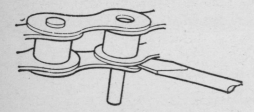

or simply twist the chain, being careful that you do not bend the plates. To replace rivet, reverse tool:

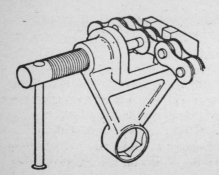

Again, be careful of how far you go, or the link will jam. Very useful for this problem (which is common) is a chain tool with a spreader slot:

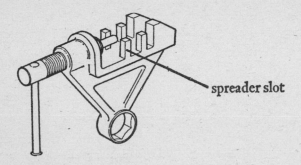

spreader slot

Fitting

Most new chains need to be shortened in order to fit properly. On a non-derailleur bike it should be set so that there is $\frac{1}{2}$-in up and down play in the chain with the rear wheel in position:

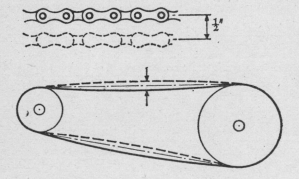

On a derailleur bike, the chain needs to be long enough to fit over the large front and back sprockets, and short enough to fit on the small front and rear sprockets. The less tension the better, but be careful that the derailleur does not double up on itself. Remove links from end of chain that has two plates with no roller between them. Some adjustment can be made by changing wheel position with the adjustable blocks on the rear drop-outs:

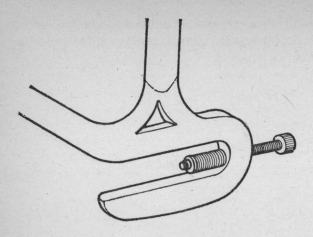

Lubrication

The best chain lubricant is LPS-3. It is easy to apply, does not attract dirt, and displaces water. Apply every two weeks, and remove and soak the chain clean in solvent every three or four months. Dry thoroughly before re-spraying.

Oil is the common lubricant. The problem is that it attracts grit and the solution is to add more oil in the hope that it will float the grit away. Oil every link once a week if your bike is in hard service, once every two weeks if it is in ordinary service. Remove and soak the chain clean in solvent once every one or two months. Let it dry thoroughly before re-oiling.

Rear sprocket/freewheel

On 1- and 3-speed bicycles the rear sprocket needs no special attention. Derailleur equipped bicycles use several sprockets (also called *cogs*) mounted on a freewheel. The insides of this mechanism are a clever maze of ball bearings, pins, springs and other minute and complex parts. Any servicing should be left to a cycle shop.

Lubricate freewheels bi-weekly with LPS-3, or once a month with oil, and remove and soak clean in solvent once a year. Removal requires a freewheel remover. There are two types, pronged and splined:

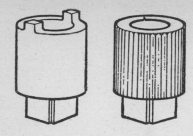

Look at your freewheel to see which you need. Remove wheel (pp. 128–31). Remove nut and washers from freewheel side of axle. Quick release hubs: remove conical nut and spring from shaft of skewer and place in a jar. Fit freewheel remover. If it won't go on, you may have a spacer nut. Remove with a wrench while holding axle stationary with another wrench on the left-side cone or locknut. Fit freewheel remover into slots or splines. Replace nut on axle or skewer and screw down hand-tight. Use a wrench on the freewheel remover to break the freewheel loose (anti-clockwise). This may be difficult. As soon as it comes loose, remove freewheel remover and spin freewheel off by hand.

Replacing freewheel: *Note:* a set of new sprockets requires a matching new chain. To replace a freewheel, grease threads and screw on carefully hand-tight. It will tighten fully as you ride.

To change a sprocket you need a sprocket remover (cycle shops). Follow directions given with the one you buy. Unless you need to change sprockets often, I suggest leaving this job to a cycle shop.

Gear change systems

Multi-speed hubs
Adjustment

Three-speed hubs: To adjust the hub, first run the shift lever
to 3rd (H). Then take up slack in cable by loosening locknut
A and screwing down barrel sleeve adjuster B:

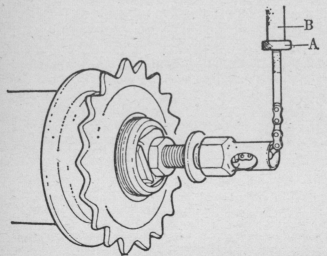

Leave cable slightly slack. If barrel sleeve cannot take up
enough slack, move the fulcrum clip which holds the cable
housing on the bike frame forward:

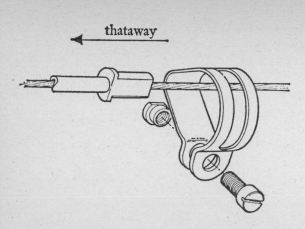

thataway

Test gears. If still not satisfactory, check position of the indicator rod by looking through the hole in the side of the right hub nut. With the shift lever in 2nd (N) position, it should be exactly even with the end of the axle:

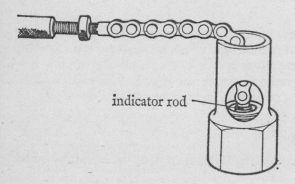

indicator rod

Adjust if necessary with the barrel sleeve. Test gears. Still no good? Remove barrel sleeve altogether. Check that indicator rod is screwed finger-tight fully into hub. Reassemble and adjust as per above. Still no? Turn to Repair, p. 152.

Five-speed hubs: For the right-hand shift lever, follow the same procedure as for the 3-speed hub, above.

For left-hand shift lever, set it all the way forward and screw cable connector into bellcrank B two or three turns:

Then run shift lever all the way back, and take slack out of cable with cable connector. Secure with locknut C.

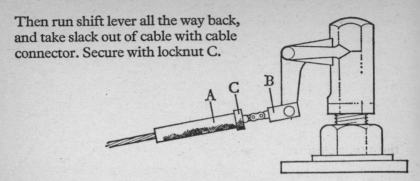

Lubrication

A teaspoonful of cycle oil, or motorists' SAE 30 oil, inside hub once a month. Do not use 'Three-in-One' or other household oils, as these leave behind a sticky residue when the oil evaporates. Once a month use a few drops of LPS or oil on the trigger control, cable and inside the cable housing.

Disassembly

Forget it. This unit is complicated. Even cycle shops generally refuse to dismantle a multi-gear hub, and instead recommend replacement. Hub failure is usually the result of using household oils which gum up the works. A hub regularly lubricated with the correct type of oil should last for the life of your bicycle.

Cable replacement

The cable wants replacing if it is frayed, or the housing kinked or broken:

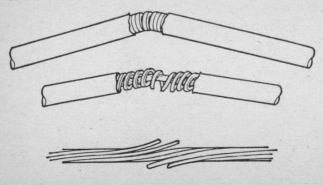

Run shift selector to 3rd (H).
Disconnect barrel sleeve from
indicator and loosen fulcrum clip (for
illustrations, see *Adjustment* above).
To free cable from a

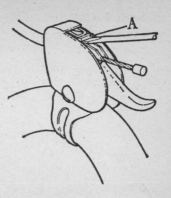

◉ Trigger: shift to 1st (L), prise up
holding plate A with a small
screwdriver, and push cable in until
the nipple clears ratchet plate:

and then pull the cable out. Remove entire cable and housing
assembly from bike and set aside fulcrum sleeve.
◉ Twist-grip: first take off the spring S with a screwdriver:

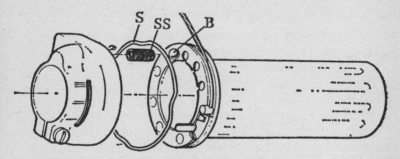

slide the twist-grip off the handlebar and catch the ball bearing
B and spring SS if they fall out. Release nipple from slot, and
remove cable and cable housing assembly from bike.
◉ Top tube lever:
undo the cable anchor bolt
near the hub:

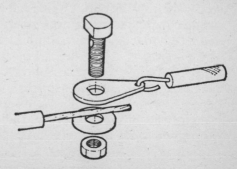

Unscrew the two shift lever halves A and B, and lift casing C
away from bike:

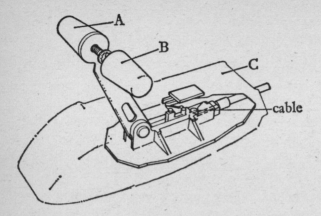

Push cable in to free nipple from slot and thread out cable.

Note: Take the old cable with you to the shop when buying
replacement. This kind of cable comes in a variety of lengths.

To replace a cable to a

⊙ Trigger: place the fulcrum sleeve on cable housing and
thread through fulcrum clip. Prise up trigger control plate,
insert cable through hole in trigger casing, and slip nipple into
slot on ratchet. Run cable over pulley wheel if you have one,
and attach to toggle chain. Shift to 3rd (H). Position fulcrum
clip so cable is just slightly slack and fix down. Adjust if
necessary as per above.

⊙ Twist-grip: insert nipple into slot. Grease and replace
spring and ball bearing. Slide twist-grip on handlebar and
secure with spring clip. Use a small screwdriver to work the
spring clip in. Run cable over pulley wheel if you have one,
and attach to toggle chain. Shift selector to 3rd (H) and adjust
as per above.

⊙ Top tube lever: thread cable through slot until nipple
catches. Replace cable housing or run cable over pulley wheel,
depending on the kind of system you have. Connect cable to
anchor bolt, shift to 3rd (H), and adjust as per above. Replace
casing, and screw together handle halves.

Shift control

If you have a damaged shift control that sticks, the best thing is to replace it. Shift controls are not expensive. Disconnect the cable (see above) and undo bolt B:

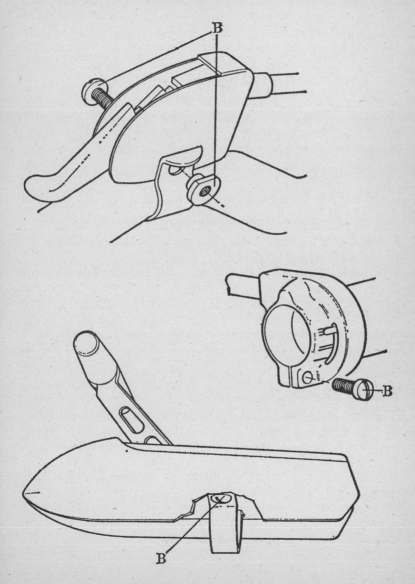

Repair

No gear at all (pedals spin freely) or slips in and out of gear.

⊙ Is gear in proper adjustment (pp. 146–48)?

⊙ Is cable binding? Check by disconnecting barrel sleeve at hub (p. 147) and working cable back and forth through the housing. Replace (pp. 148–50) if it binds.

⊙ Is shift mechanism together and functioning? Stick and twist-grip models are especially prone to slippage after the track for the ball bearing becomes worn:

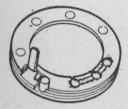

⊙ The insides of the hub may be clogged through the use of household or too heavy oils. Try putting in LPS, paraffin, or penetrating oil and jiggling everything around. No?

⊙ Give up. Remove wheel (pp. 128–31) and take to a bike shop.

Derailleurs

A derailleur system includes a shift lever, cable and front or rear derailleur.

Shift levers

The shift lever should be set so that you can move it without undue strain, but be stiff enough to hold fast against spring pressure from the derailleur. This adjustment is made with the tension screw A:

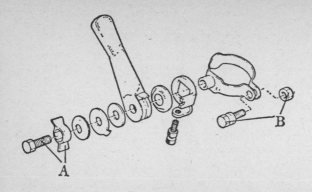

Some tension screws have a slot for a screwdriver (or coin), others have wings, and others have wire loops. All function the same way. Do not lubricate the shift lever.

Cables

Adjustment: Cables for a derailleur system wear rapidly. Check them often for fraying:

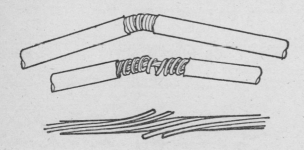

Adjustment is needed when the shift lever has to be pulled all the way back to engage the large sprocket. Place the shift lever forward so the chain is on the smallest sprocket. Some systems have a barrel adjuster, either at the derailleur or at the shift lever:

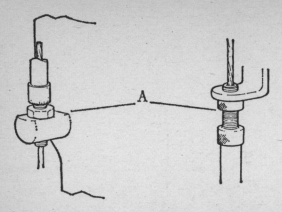

Undo the locknut A and move the barrel adjuster up until slack is moved from the cable. If this will not do the job, turn barrel adjuster back down fully home, and reset the cable anchor bolt.

All derailleurs, front and back, use a cable anchor bolt or screw to hold the cable. Here is the location (CB) on two representative types:

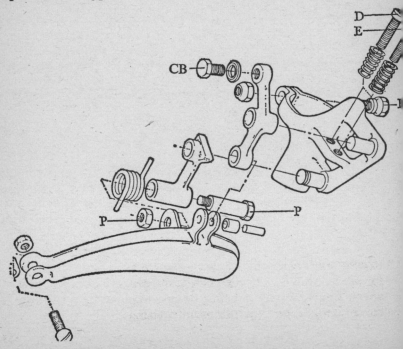

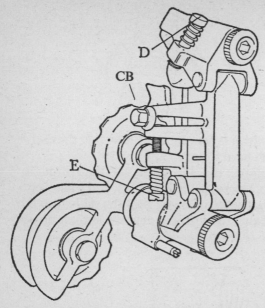

Loosen the bolt, take the slack out of the cable, pulling it through with pliers if necessary, and re-tighten bolt.

Removal and replacement: Run chain to smallest sprocket. Screw home barrel adjuster, if you have one. Undo cable anchor bolt and thread cable out of derailleur. Check cable housings (not used on all models) for kinks and breaks. Remove cable from lever by threading it out:

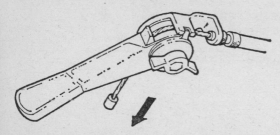

Reassembly: *Note:* do not cut new cable to size until it is installed or it will jam when going into cable housings. If you are cutting new cable housing, be sure to place the jaws of the cutter *between* the wire coils of the housing:

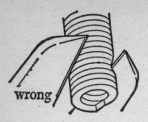
wrong

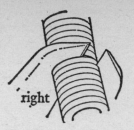
right

and finish the job off with a taper ream or file so that the end of the housing does not have a burr.

Thread the cable through the shift lever, and then through down tube tunnel, cable stops, cable housings, and whatever else is in your particular system. As you pass the cable through the cable housings, be sure to twist it so that the strands do not unravel:

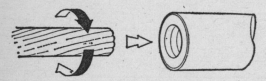

Finish at derailleur. Move shift lever to forward position, make sure that cable housing ferrules (if you have them) are seated properly, and attach cable to cable anchor bolt.

Front derailleur

Adjustment: The changer as a whole must be properly positioned, with the outer side of the cage about $\frac{1}{4}$ in to $\frac{1}{2}$ in above the sprocket:

$\frac{1}{4}" - \frac{1}{2}"$

Raise or lower the unit by undoing the mounting bolt B. The sides of the cage should follow the curvature of the sprocket. Some cages are adjustable in this respect, others (perfectly good ones) are not. Those that are usually swivel on a post between the cage and changer. Sometimes the post comes off the changer, and sometimes off the cage. Either way, there will be a locking bolt like C:

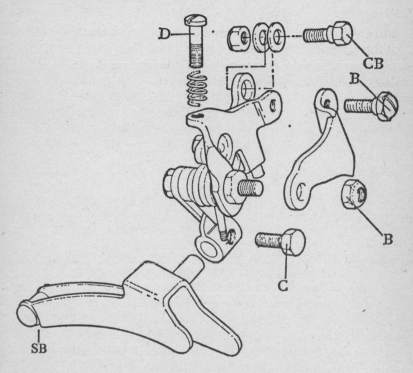

Loosen bolt C, rotate cage to desired position, tighten.

Side to side travel of the cage must be set. First check that the cable is properly adjusted (pp. 153–55). Front derailleurs come with either one or two adjusting screws. Look at yours to determine the type.

One-screw derailleurs: Run the chain to largest back and smallest front sprockets. The first adjustment is made with the cage positioning bolt C (above). Loosen it, and move the cage so that the left side just clears the chain.

Tighten bolt C. Now loosen the adjusting bolt or screw D three or four turns. Run the chain to the smallest back and largest front sprockets. Using the shift lever, position the cage so that the right side just clears the chain. Turn down adjusting screw D until resistance is felt, and stop. Test gears. Often several fine adjustments will be necessary before they work perfectly.

Two-screw derailleurs: If you can't find your adjusting screws easily, get down close to the unit and watch it carefully as you wiggle the shift lever back and forth. Each time the body of the changer reaches the end of its travel it will be resting on a spring-loaded screw or knurled ring:

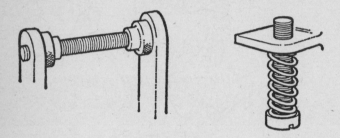

On Campagnolo units they are the screws E and D (opposite): Run chain to largest back and smallest front sprockets. It should just clear the left side of the cage. Adjust left side adjusting screw D as necessary until it does. Now run chain to smallest back and largest front sprockets. It should just clear the right side of the cage. Adjust right side adjusting screw E as necessary until it does. Test gears. Sometimes it is necessary to set the high gear adjustment a little wide to make the chain climb up on the big sprocket – but be cautious, or the chain will throw off the sprocket.

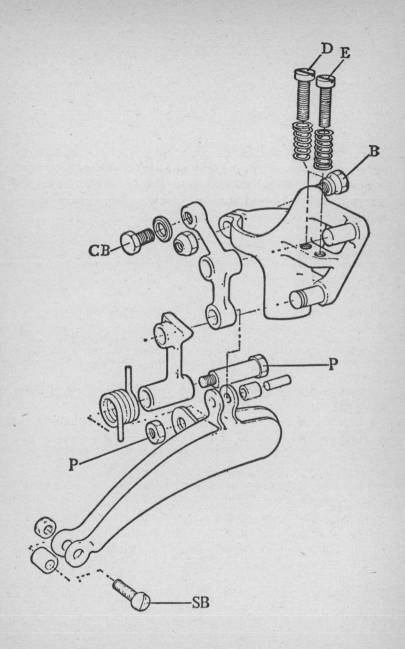

Lubrication

A little LPS or a few drops of oil on the pivot bolts once a month.
If the unit becomes particularly dirty take it off by undoing
the cable anchor bolt CB, spacer bolt SB, and then mounting
bolt(s) B (see previous illustrations), and soak it clean in solvent.

Repair

Most of the difficulties experienced with the front changer are
actually caused by problems elsewhere in the power train.
This checklist assumes that you have already set your changer
as per Adjustment, pp. 156–59.

Chain rubs side of cage

⊙ Is shift lever tight (pp. 152–53) ?
⊙ Can you stop the rubbing by diddling with the shift lever ?
For example, the amount of travel in the cage necessary to
make the chain climb from the small to the large sprocket may
leave the cage too far to the right and cause the chain to rub
the left side of the cage. It is frequently necessary with front
changers to move the cage back to the left just a trifle after
shifting to the large front sprocket.
⊙ Is the sprocket warped or loose ?

Chain throws off sprocket

⊙ Is shift lever tight (pp. 152–53) ?
⊙ Cage travel may be too far out. Adjust slightly (pp. 157–59).
⊙ Is chain old ? Test (p. 141).
⊙ Are sprocket teeth bent ?
⊙ Are front and rear sprockets in alignment ?
⊙ Try using an adjustable end spanner to bend the leading tip
of the outside cage in very slightly – about $\frac{1}{16}$ in:

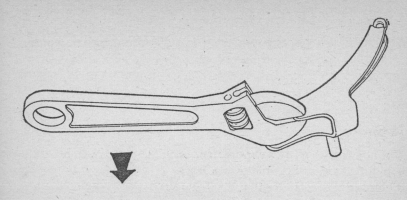

Delayed shifts or no shifts at all

⊙ Are pivot bolts clean ? Try a little LPS or oil.
⊙ Is spring intact and in place ?
⊙ Is cable sticking or broken (pp. 153–56) ?

Rear derailleur

Adjustment: Side to side travel: set chain on smallest rear and biggest front sprockets, with gear shift lever all the way forward, and check that there is only a little slack in the cable. Adjust if necessary with barrel adjuster and/or cable anchor bolt (pp. 154–55).

The derailleur needs to be set so that side to side travel is stopped short of throwing the chain into the wheel or off the small sprocket. This is done with two adjusting screws or knurled rings, and here is their location on three typical units (high gear – E, low gear – D):

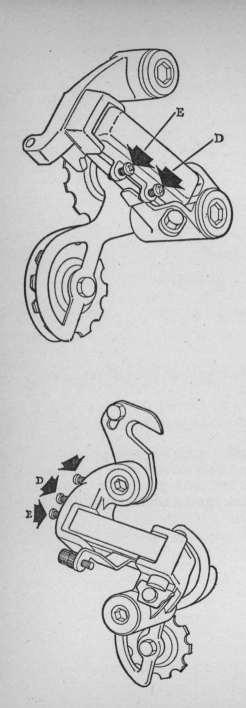

D   E

If your derailleur isn't included here, get down close to it and run it back and forth, seeing which adjusting screw does what. OK, now: if derailleur goes too far, throwing chain off, set in position with shift lever so that jockey wheel lines up with the sprocket on the side that you are working on, and turn in the appropriate adjusting screw or knurled ring until resistance is felt. Stop. If derailleur does not go far enough, back the appropriate screw off until it does. If this does not work, turn to *Repair*, below.

Repair

Derailleur is sticky, won't always shift, sometimes shifts unexpectedly

◉ Is shift lever working smoothly but with enough friction to hold derailleur in place (pp. 152–53)?

◉ Are cables sticking (pp. 153–56)?

◉ Are pivot bolts lubricated and clean? On some models (Campagnolo, Huret, among others) these bolts can be adjusted:

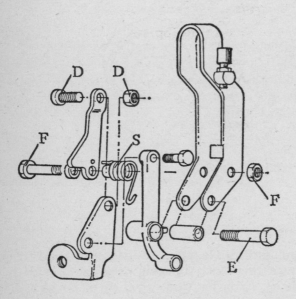

Undo locknuts for bolts D, E, and F, undo bolts one-eighth turn and reset locknuts.

Derailleur will not go far enough

◉ Is cable slightly slack with shift lever all the way forward (pp. 152–53)?

◉ Are adjusting screws properly set (pp. 161–63)?

◉ Is the cable able to slide freely (pp. 153–56)?

◉ Is pivot or main changer spring broken?

◉ Are chain rollers lined up with chain?

◉ Try to wiggle the derailleur unit by hand. Can you push it to the desired position?

Yes: the works are gummed up. Dismantle, clean in solvent, and lubricate with LPS or oil. Adjust pivot bolts, if possible (see above).

No: if it won't reach the big rear sprocket, remove mounting plate and bend it in a vice. Do the same if it won't reach the little rear sprocket, or put in shims at the mounting bolt.

Chain throws off sprockets

◉ Are adjusting screws set correctly (pp. 161–63)?
◉ Are any teeth worn or bent?
◉ Is the chain good (p. 141)?
◉ If chain is skipping, is spring tension for roller cage sufficient?
◉ Is roller cage aligned with chain?

Power train repair index
Noises

First make sure that the noise is coming from the power train by coasting the bike. If the noise continues it is probably a brake or hub problem.

Determine if the noise comes from the front (crankset), the chain, or the rear freewheel. Do this by disconnecting the chain and spinning the various parts.

Grinding noises

Front:
◎ Check bottom bracket bearings (pp. 138–39) and pedal bearings (p. 135).
◎ Is chain rubbing derailleur? Or is front sprocket rubbing cage or chainstays?
Back:
◎ Wheel bearings OK (pp. 131–33)?
◎ Freewheel OK (pp. 144–45)?

Clicks or clunks

One for every revolution of crankset:
◎ Are pedals tight (p. 135)?
◎ Are cranks tight (pp. 136–38)?
◎ Bottom bracket bearings OK (pp. 138–39)?
◎ Are any teeth on the sprocket(s) bent?
Two or three for every revolution of the crankset:
◎ Are any teeth on the rear sprockets bent?
◎ Is chain worn or jammed up?

For all other problems consult the Repair section for the part which is not functioning.

See overleaf for service chart

Service interval chart

Part	Weekly	Bi-weekly	Monthly	Bi-monthly	3 months	6 months	Yearly
General	Clean with cloth and toothbrush		Nuts and bolts secure ?			Wax or coat with LPS-1	Leather saddles, dress with neatsfoot oil from underneath
Tyres	Check pressure and for embedded glass						
Brakes	Check cable and shoe adjustment		Oil or LPS pivot bolt adjustment				Dismantle, clean and regrease
Rims	Check for truth and even spoke tension						
Chain	Oil, if in hard service	Oil, if in normal service LPS-3	Check for play	Remove, clean and re-oil	Remove, clean and re-LPS-3		

Component			
Derailleurs	Oil or LPS	Chain roller wheels – dismantle, clean and regrease	Dismantle, clean and regrease or LPS
3-speed hub	Oil		
Hubs	Oil, check adjustment	Dismantle, clean, regrease	
Bottom bracket	Oil, check adjustment	Dismantle, clean, and regrease (hard service)	Dismantle, clean and regrease (ordinary service)
Headset	Check adjustment		
Pedals	Oil, check adjustment		
Cables	Check for fraying	Oil or LPS-3	Dismantle and regrease or LPS

12 Curious and unusual velocipedes

Man-powered vehicles are called velocipedes, and are a recent invention. Although the wheel was in use by the Sumerians as long ago as 3500 BC, and there are hints in old Egyptian and Chinese artwork of simple velocipedes, we know of no ancient civilizations that had anything even resembling a bicycle.

The papers of Leonardo da Vinci include sketches of what appears to be a bicycle. And the stained glass window at the church of Stoke Poges in England, built in 1642, includes what may have been a bicycle.

But the first ancestor of the bicycle to actually be built was shown at the Palais Royal, Paris, by Comte de Sivrac in 1791:

Almost certainly inspired by a child's toy, the celerifère was pushed with the feet, like a scooter. From this simple beginning, development of the bicycle was extraordinarily swift. In 1817 Baron von Drais invented the Draisienne, later called 'hobbyhorse', which featured a frame and steering:

In 1839 a British inventor named Kirkpatrick Macmillan devised a treadle system of pedals:

And in 1861 came the Michaux Velocipede, which featured a pedal driven front wheel:

Called a 'boneshaker' in England, this bicycle led naturally to the ordinary or 'penny-farthing':

Finally, in 1884 James Starley introduced the forerunner of today's bicycle, the Rover Safety, with a chain drive:

THE ROVER SAFETY
BICYCLE (PATENTED).

Safer than any Tricycle, faster and easier than any Bicycle ever made. Fitted with handles to turn for convenience in storing or shipping. Far and away the best hill-climber in the market.

The 'Safety' was far and away the most practical type of bicycle, and by 1890 was the standard design. But in the years 1860 to 1890 it had been preceded by many highly interesting experimental designs and innovations.

Machines like the Royal Salvo (1877)
were something to behold:

But perhaps the most amusing was the Gibbons Pentacycle (1881), fondly known as 'Hen-and-Chickens':
The Post Office put a number of these machines into use for delivering parcels, but found them impractical. On the rough roads of the day the main driving wheel would often lose contact with the ground, leaving the rider pedalling uselessly!

Imaginative inventors extended the use of bicycle design.
One fine July day in 1883 a Mr Terry, having cycled down to
Dover from London earlier in the week, rode out to the beach.
With the aid of some canvas and rod he then transformed his
tricycle into a boat, hopped in, and rowed across the Channel,
arriving at Andreselles, in France the next morning!

A few months later Mr Terry
devised another aquatic design:

Mr Terry was not alone, for other inventors devised similar machines:

Other innovations included a steam bicycle:

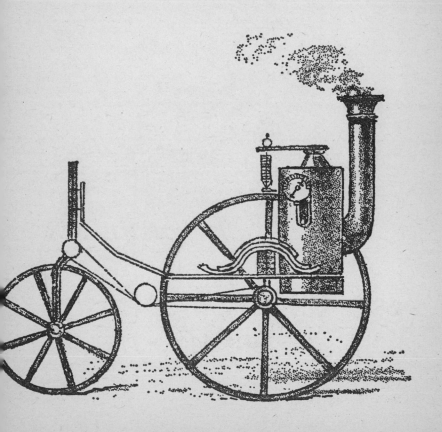

A bicycle for riding on ice:

The bicycle went to war.
Troops mounted on folding bicycles
were formed:

And bicycles were used to mount machine-guns:

There were sailing bicycles:

And man even built bicycles to fly.

And now, today, with the renewed interest in velocipedes as inexpensive, convenient transportation, inventors are working on new designs:

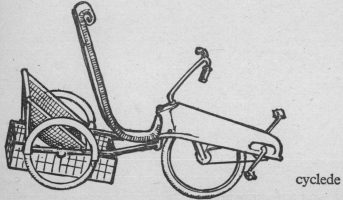

cyclede

There is considerable interest in what are now called PPVs—People Powered Vehicles. Inventors and manufacturers are trying to solve the problems of inclement weather and carrying capacity. A number of firms are producing 2-seater quadricycles with convertible tops. These vehicles are useful for shopping and for when it rains, but the main means of transportation in the future is – the bicycle!

Index

Noel Lloyd and Jennifer Laing
The Young Archaeologist's Handbook 40p

Archaeology? Why not have a go?

This is an unusual book which shows you how to make a 'find' and document it, how to plan an expedition, how to use the museums, and what to look out for in town and in the countryside.

Anthony Greenbank
Survival for Young People 45p

Anyone, any time, can be faced with an emergency indoors or out, for example:

a fire traps you in a room
someone is drowning
you are lost in unknown territory
you capsize your boat

Would you know what to do? Read this book and you will be prepared for most of them – in fact you might be able to prevent some.

You can buy these and other Piccolo books from booksellers and newsagents: or direct from the following address:
Pan Books, Cavaye Place, London SW10 9PG
Send purchase price plus 15p for the first book and 5p for each additional book to allow for postage and packing
Prices quoted are applicable in UK
While every effort is made to keep prices low, it is sometimes necessary to increase prices at short notice. Pan books reserve the right to show on covers new retail prices which may differ from those advertised in the text or elsewhere